ENCYCLOPAEDIA OF INDIAN GOVERNMENT: PROGRAMMES AND POLICIES

ENCYCLOPAEDIA
OF
INDIAN GOVERNMENT:
PROGRAMMES AND POLICIES

Vol. 4

Agriculture and Food Processing

Edited by

Satish Tiwari

ANMOL PUBLICATIONS PVT. LTD.

NEW DELHI - 110 002 (INDIA)

ANMOL PUBLICATIONS PVT. LTD.
4374/4B, Ansari Road, Daryaganj
New Delhi - 110 002

Encyclopaedia of Indian Government: Programmes and Policies

First Edition, 2000

ISBN 81-261-0515-1 (Set)

[Responsibility for the facts stated, opinions expressed, conclusions reached and plagiarism, if any, in these volumes is entirely that of the Editor. The Publisher bears no responsibility for them whatsoever.]

PRINTED IN INDIA

Published by J.L. Kumar for Anmol Publications Pvt. Ltd., New Delhi - 110 002 and Printed at Mehra Offset Press, Delhi.

Contents

	Preface	*vii*
1.	Organisation	1
2.	Agriculture and Allied Sectors	10
3.	Approach and Strategies	103
4.	Animal Husbandry	114
5.	Food Processing Industries	145
6.	Diary Development	151
7.	Fisheries	163
8.	Plan Schemes, Special Component Plan	
9.	Tribal Sub Plan	176
10.	Promotion of Food Processing	186
11.	Promotional Support	189
12.	R & D Human Resource Development	197
13.	Food Safety & Quality	201
14.	Public Sector Enterprise	206
15.	Future Developments	214

Preface

Encyclopaedia of Indian Government: Programmes and Policies contains authoritative information on about fifty departmental policies and their future developmental programmes.

Organised to be completed in 40 volumes, this gigantic work covers Agriculture; Atomic Energy; Chemicals and Fertilizers; Coal; Commerce; Communication; Culture; Defence; Education; Environment and Forests; External Affairs; Finance; Food & Consumer Affairs; Food Processing Industries; Health and Family Welfare; Home Affairs and Internal Security; Human Resources; Industry; Information and Broadcasting; Labour; Law, Justice and Company Affairs; Non-conventional Energy Sources; Ocean Development; Parliamentary Affairs; Personnel, Public Grievances and Pensions; Petroleum and Natural Gas; Planning and Programme Implementation; Planning and Statistics; Posts and Telegraphs; Power; Rural Development; Science and Technology; Social Justice and Empowerment; Space; States Affairs; Steel; Steel and Mines; Sugar and Edible Oils; Surface Transport; Textiles; Tourism; Urban Development; Water Resources; Women and Child development etc.

Based on the information derived from authoritative sources, this work contains authentic facts and figures. I am deeply beholden to all the scholars whose writings are cited or substantially made use of in the present work. I am also thankful to Anmol Publications Pvt. Ltd. for undertaking publication of this encyclopaedia. I am solely responsible for shortcomings in presentation of matter.

Encyclopaedic in nature, this will prove a dependable reference work for scholars and academics besides those appearing for different competitive examinations.

—**Satish Tiwari**

1

Organisation

The Department of Animal Husbandry and Dairying (AH&D) is one of the Departments in the Ministry of Agriculture, and came into existence w.e.f. 1st February, 1991, by converting two divisions of the Department of the Agriculture and Cooperation namely Animal Husbandry and Dairy Development into a separate Department. The Fisheries Division of the Department of Agriculture and Cooperation and a part of the Ministry of Food Processing Industries were later transferred to the Department of Animal Husbandry & Dairying w.e.f. 10th October, 1997. Shri Som Pal is the Minister of State while the Prime Minister is the Minister.

The administrative head of the Department is the Secretary, Animal Husbandry and Dairying. Shri N.K. Shina, has taken over charge as Secretary (AH&D) w.e.f. 20th November, 1997.

Functions

The Department is responsible for matters relating to livestock production, preservation, protection and improvement of stocks and dairy development including Technology Mission on Dairy Development, and also for matters relating to the Delhi Milk Scheme and the National Dairy Development Board. It also looks after all matters pertaining to fishing and fisheries, inland and marine.

The Department advises State Governments/ Union Territories in the formulation of policies and programmes in the field of Animal Husbandry and Dairy Development and Fisheries. The main focus of ' the activities is on (a) development of requisite infrastructure in States/UTs for improving animal productivity (b) preservation and protection of livestock through provision of health care (c) strengthening of Central livestock farms (Cattle, Sheep and Poultry) for development of superior germ plasm for distribution of states and (d) expansion of Aquaculture in fresh brackish water, and welfare of fisherfolk etc.

Subordinate offices

The animal husbandry division deals with as many as 9 disciplines and looks after administration of the 44 field offices/subordinate offices spread over the country.

National Dairy Development Board (NDDB)

The National Dairy Development Board is a premier institution, and is located at Anand, Gujarat. The Board was set up in 1965 to accelerate the pace of dairy development on cooperative lines.

Dr. V. Kurien had been the Chairman of the National Dairy Development Board since its inception. Following his resignation (Dr. (Ms.) Amrita Patel has been appointed the Chairman with effect from 26 November, 1998.

Advisory boards

Seven Advisory Committees/Councils/ Boards have been constituted to advise the Department for promotion of activities in Various fields of animal husbandry and fisheries sectors. These are:

(i) Gosamvardhan Advisory Council;

(ii) Central Advisory Committee for Development of Sheep, Goats and Rabbits;

(iii) Equine Development Board;

(iv) Central Poultry Development Advisiory Council;

(v) Milk and Milk Product Advisory Board;

(vi) Central Board of Fisheries;

(vii) Veterinary Council of India.

Staff grievance cell

A Staff Grievances Cell has been established in the Department to look into grievances. Action has also been initiated to extend this facility to subordinate offices of the Department.

Liaison officer for SC/ST

An officer in the rank of Deputy Secretary in the Department has been designated as Liaison Officer for SC/ST employees. Action has also been taken to extend the facility to subordinate offices.

Vigilance unit

A Vigilance Unit has been functioning in the Department to process vigilance cases pertaining to the department and subordinate offices including DMS and NDDB.

Progressive use of Hindi

During the year under review, concrete efforts were made by the Department for promotion of Hindi in official work. The Hindi section was actively involved in translating various important documents as well as in implementing the Official Language policy of the Government.

An Official Language Implementation Committee is functioning in the Department under the Chairmanship of a Joint Secretary. In accordance with the prescribed rules, regular meetings of the Committee were held during the year. The progress in use of Hindi in the

Department was reviewed in these meetings and programmes were formulated to achieve better results.

As per directions of the Department of Official Language, a Hindi forthnight was organised in the Department for the first time from 1st to 15th September, 1998. The Hon'ble Minister of State for Agriculture issued an appeal on this occasion requesting all concerned to do their maximum work in Hindi. Various competitions were also held during this fortnight wherein a large number of officials participated. The successful officials were given cash awards and certificates in a function chaired by the Joint Secretary.

An Annual Action Programme has been formulated for promoting Hindi. In pursuance of orders of the Department of Official Language and with a view to assess the progress of Hindi in subordinate offices. Deputy Secretary (Administration) and Assistant Director (OL) inspected the offices located at Calcutta, Cochin and Mumbai.

During the period of report, Assistant Director (OL) was deputy to the All India Official Language Conference organised by the Rashtriya Hindi Academy, Rupambara from 2nd to 4th October, 1998 in Shimla.

Publicity/communications

The Department of Animal Husbandry and Dairying has been working closely with the Ministry of Information and Broadcasting for a multimedia campaign to highlight achievements, create awareness, educate, and motivate people about programmes in the livestock sector.

Secretary (AH&D) is a member of the National Level Media Coordination Committee constituted under the Chairmanship of Secretary, Department of Agriculture and Cooperation. A representative of the Department is included in the core group constituted for coordination of various activities. Officers of the Department are members of media level Sub-Committees on Doordarshan, All India Radio and Field Publicity constituted in May, 1994.

Wide press and media publicity of the programmes of animal husbandry and dairying was organised through the Press Information Bureau of the Ministry of Information and Broadcasting.

Computerised information system

The Department has developed a computerised information system, with the help of NIC unit to accelerate the flow of information generated. This also assists in planning, policy formulation, monitoring and preparation of projects for rapid development of the sector.

Software packages have been developed for computerisation of information generated under various schemes of the Department. All officers, PAs and staff have been provided short duration training on computer operations to develop a computer culture in the Department.

Besides, computer terminals have been provided in the rooms of officers to provide access to database and other relevant information.

Electronic Mail facility has been extended to all users. Apart from E-mail, other facilities available on INTERNET have also been provided.

A Facilitation counter is functioning is Krishi Bhavan which offers relevant information to the general public.

National task force

A National Task Force has been constituted under the chairmanship of Secretary (AH&D) ti monitor and strengthen the NICNET base, Integrated Animal

Husbandry and Dairying Information System at District/ State/Central level.

International cooperation

Shri Babu Jacob. Joint Secretary was deputed to attend the International Agricultural Fair 1998 held at Paris, France during 3-8th March 1998.

A delegation, comprising Shri Ujagar Sing Director and Dr. K.R. Viswanathan, Deputy Commissioner (Livestock Health) was deputed f visiting Vietnam to study goat development ai related activities during 18—24th March. 1998.

Dr. Y.S. Yadava, FDC and Shri J.P.S. Mehrotra, Deputy Commissioner (Fisheries) were deputed to attend the Regional Workshop Monitoring & Evaluation and Impact Assesment Fisheries Development and Management held from 23-26th March, 1998 and the 23rd meeting Advisory Committee of Bay of Bengal Program held in Sri Lanka During 27-28th March, 11 respectively.

A delegation consisting of Shri N. Rama Rao, Joint Secretary and Shri K. Omprakash

Director, CICEF, Bangalore had visited Japan from 31.3.98 to 10.4.98 to attend the tender opening, evaluation of the tenders, and the signing of contract for procurement of Dredger under Japan grant-in-aid programme.

Dr. Y.S. Yadava, FDC was deputed to attend Regional Conference for Asia and Pacific held in Yangon. Myanmar during 20-24th April, 1998.

Dr. Y.S. Yadav, FDC was deputed to Italy to participate in the Adhoc Meeting on Indicators and Criteria of Sustainable Shrimp Culture held in Rome at FAO HQS during 28-30 April, 1998.

Shri Babu Jacob, Joint Secretary, Shri I.K. Narang,

6

Dairy Development

The importance of dairying lies not only in the production of milk and milk products but the fact that it brings about significant changes in the socioeconomic structure of the rural economy. Its role in employment generation is well recognised. The primary objective of dairying is generating additional income for the resource-poor farmers producting milk in villages.

With a view to acclerate progress and rapid development of this sector, the Department of Animal Husbandry and Dairying implemented a total of 4 Plan Schemes in dairy development sector during 1998-99. The progress and achievement made under these schemes is highlighted below.

Operation Flood (Completed)

The National Dairy Development Board (NDDB). Was set up by the Government of India an institution of national importance, to promote, plan and organise programmes for development of dairy and other agriculture based and allied industries along cooperative lines on an intensive and nationwide basis.

Operation Flood, an integrated dairy development programme, completed its third phase on April 30, 1996. The main thrust of the programme was to consolidate the gains already achieved, and to strengthen the dairy cooperative structure for sustainable development of the dairy industry in India. At the end of Phase 3, there was a balance of Rs. 34 crores out of the EEC contribution to the OF project. The EEC approved utilisation of these funds on the following two major components:

(1) Women Dairy Cooperative Leadership Development Project

(2) Strengthening of Dairy Cooperatives to meet he competitive challenges of the next decade.

These components are primarily aimed at strengthening cooperatives at the grassroot level. The programme Implementation Agreement (PIA) was signed between the EEC and the NDDB and was endorsed by the Govt. of India on August 21. 1997 Consequently measures were initiated from September, 1997 and are continuing during 1998-99.

Women dairy cooperative leadership programme (WDCLP)

The project aims at nurturing leadership amongst women dairy farmers for economic and social empowerment besides ensuring their say in the governance of dairy cooperatives. Major subcomponents of project activities include identifying staff for carrying out training activities, developing communication strategies, organising, educating and training women dairy farmers and initiating group activities for income generation and thrift. During 1998-99 the programme was initiated in 11 milk unions. In each union the programme is being implemented in 20-25 village dairy cooperatives.

Strengthening of dairy cooperatives to meet competitive challenges of the next decade

The different sub-components and the proposed activities of the programme are as follows:

(i) Cooperative institution building programme:

The project would focus on the emergence of a well-informed constituency of members, responsive managing committee members of the village dairy cooperative societies, a proactive board of directors of milk unions, committed cooperators as well as competent and responsible staff. During the year 1998-99, the programme was initiated in 8 milk unions.

(ii) Information support system

It is proposed to initiate an information system involving Geographical Information System (GIS) in 18 unions and annual outlay of Rs. 45 lakhs. The GIS would provide decision support and aid in strategic planning in areas of milk procurement, veterinary health, epidemiology, etc. It is estimated that all milk unions of Karnataka and Kerala and three more unions in Rajasthan and two unions in Punjab will be included this year.

(iii) Management development (competence building):

The basic purpose of this component is to enhance efficiency of professional staff employed by cooperatives. It would involve various training programmes in areas of participatory rural appraisal training on animal husbandry practices.

(iv) Marketing support:

This programme aims at increasing the sale of milk and fresh milk products of dairy cooperatives through building image of products, consumer orientation and brand awareness programmes. It initiates active generic promotion campaign. A sum of Rs. 50.52 lakh was utilised on generic promotion campaign and a sum of Rs. 73.67 lakhs involving some 28 milk Unions has been utilised by October 1998, on skill-building.

(v) Monitoring & research

The programme aims at generating adequate information in areas of consumer market research and milk procurement market so as to make dairy cooperatives more market-competitive. About 11 rural studies and 8 urban have been initiated involving an outlay of Rs. 50 lakh as on September, 1998. -

DCS Organisaiton and Membership

By September 1998. 78945, (estimated) Anand pattern dairy cooperative societies were organised in 170 milksheds involving about 100 lakh farmer members.

Milk Procurement, Processing and Marketing:

The average milk procurement during April - October, 1998 was 121.6 lakh kg/day. 6 per cent higher than in the last year. It is expected that average milk procurement during the current year would be about 5 per cent more than during 1997-98.

Till October' 98, about 118.2 lakh litres/day of milk was marketed as against 111.4 lakh litres/day during the corresponding period last year, reflecting a growth of 6 per cent. Cooperatives are marketing liquid milk in over 700 urban centres. The total rural milk processing capacity in the programme stood at 204.5 lakh litres a day with powder production capacity at 1054 MT/dsy. To minimise the adverse impact of regional and seasonal imbalances in procurement and marketing, 1142 road milk tankers and 171 rail milk tankers for long distance transportation of liquid milk have been provided.

Milk production enhancement:

By September 1998, about 37,000 societies were covered under the Animal health Programme some 27,000 had first-aid (excluding those dovetailed through- the Technology Mission on Dairy Development) facilities. About 20,000 village societies were provided with artificial insemination facilities. To improve utilisation of the available infrastructure about 1800 Cluster All centres were in operation, with each cluster meeting the requirement on an average of 5 DCS villages using frozen semen.

By March 1998 the total feed manufacturing capacity was 5205 MT/Day and the total feed manufactured was about 8.56 lakh MT.

Physical progress

Particulars	94-95	95-96	96-97	97-98	98-99
Societies organised (1000)	69.8	72.7	74.3	77.5	78.9@
Rural dairy processing capacity (lakh litres/day)	181.0	192.0	204.5	204.5	204.5@
Farmer members (lakh)	89.9	93.1	95.9	98.8	99.8@
Average rural milk procurement (lakh kgs/day)	102.8	109.4	122.6	128.9	121.6$
Liquid milk marketing (lakh litres/day)	93.9	99.4	105.1	111.3	118.2$

Assistance to cooperatives

4.8.1 the scheme is aimed at off-setting the accumulated losses incurred by Dairy Cooperatives consequent to transfer of assets and liabilities by erstwhile State Dairy Development Corporations to Dairy Cooperative Unions/Federations. Such accumulated losses have imposed severe hardships on milk producers and the dairy economy.

It was therefore felt that past accumulated losses of dairy federations/unions should he written off, so as to provide fresh start on an economically viable basis with unhindered operational freedom. The scale of their operations would also be expanded so as to benefit more farmers, once the past losses are written off, the organisations would require some time to gradually improve their performance and, in order to enable them to overcome this transitional phase, appropriate rehabilitation plans are to be worked out in each case with a mechanism for thorough appraisal and close monitoring to ensure their continued viability. The scheme has been recommended by EFC for approval.

Technology mission on dairy development:

The Technology Mission on Dairy Development launched in August 1988 aimed at supplementing and supporting efforts of the NDDB under "Operation Flood" programme and thereby enhancing rural employment opportunities and income generation through dairy development. The tenure of the Mission ended in March 1997. However it was continued on a reduced scale during 1997-98 and also 1998-99. A provision of Rs. I crore was made in the current year's budget for spill over works, which is expected to be completed by March 1999.

TMDD has taken up a pilot project for establishing Liquid nitrogen delivery systems in Gujarat and Karnataka at a cost of 460 lakhs. The LN delivery system in Karnataka has been commissioned, and the Cooperative Unions and the department of AH have started using this facility for procuring liquid nitrogen, similarly, the LN delivery system for Gujarat will become fully operational in the near future.

The TMDD has taken up a programme for producing improved fodder seeds through registered seed growers, who are members of the District Cooperative Milk Productions Unions and a few NGOs During 1998-99. 22 seed producing agencies from 11 states with financial and technical support form TMDD have targeted to produce 31000 quintals of quality fodder seeds of different varieties.

Integrated dairy development projects in non operation flood, hilly and backward areas:

An Integrated Dairy Development Programme in non-Operation Flood, Hilly and Backward areas was launched during the 8th Plan with a total outlay of Rs. 200 crores as a Central Sector Scheme. This Scheme has been extended during the current year 1998-99 with a total provision of Rs. 25.60 crores. The main objectives of the scheme are as under:-

(i) Development of milch cattle.

(ii) To increase the milk production by providing Technical Inputs services.

(iii) Procurement, processing and marketing of milk in a cost effective manner.

(iv) To ensure remunerative prices to the milk producers.

(v) To generate additional employment opportunities.

(vi) To improve social, nutritional and economic status of residents of comparatively more disadvantaged areas.

Since the starting of the scheme 38 projects with a total outlay of Rs. 189.84 crores have been sanctioned in 20 States (Arunachal Pradesh, Sikkim, Mizoram, Tripura, Gujarat, Nagaland, Orissa, Madhya Pradesh, Manipur, Uttar Pradesh, West Bengal, Meghalaya, Bihar, Assam, Andhra Pradesh, Haryana, Maharashtra, Jammu and Kashmir, Tamil Nadu and Himachal Pradesh) and one Union Territory of Andaman and Nicobar Islands. A sum of Rs. 114.81 crores has been released for IDDP Projects upto December, 1998 including a sum of Rs. 9.70 crores during the financial year 1998-99.

Upto September, 1998 over 5000 DCS have been organised under the Project with a total farmer membership of about 4.02 lakh. Three new projects in Nagaland, Orissa and West Bengal have been approved during 1998-99 with an outlay of Rs. 11.10 crore.

Milk and milk product order-1992:

4.11.1 The Government of India notified the Milk and Milk Product Order on 9.6.92. As per the provisions of this order any person/dairy plant handling more than 10.000 litres per day of milk or 500 MT milk of solids per annum, needs to be registered with the registering authority appointed by the Central Government. The Milk and Milk Product Order authorises the State Governments to register units handling upto 75.000 litres of milk per day or 3.750 MTs, of milk solids per annum. The Central Registering Authority is granting registration for units handling more than 75.000 litres of milk per day or 3.750 MTs of milk solids per annum. The Central Registering Authority has granted registration for 251 units with a combined capacity of 462.19 lakh hires per day upto December, 1998. Since the promulgation of the order, 236 applications have been rejected on various grounds, mainly, for want of surplus milk in the milkshed areas and poor hygienic and sanitary conditions in the plant or the premises.

Under MMPO a provision has been made to stregthen testing facilities for States so that necessary infrastructure can be developed. During 1998-99, a sum of Rs. 85 lakh has been released to the states against a provision of Rs. I crore.

Delhi milk scheme:

The DMS was set up in 1959 with the primary objective of supplying wholesome milk to citizens of Delhi at reasonable prices, as well as for providing remunerative prices to milk producers. The manufacture and sale of milk products like ghee, table butter and curd is also undertaken as an allied activity.

Installed capacity:

Initially the DMS was established for processing/ packaging of 2.55 lakh litres of milk per day, which has been expanded in phases to the present level of 5 lakh litres milk per day.

Management:

DMS is headed by a General Manager with powers of a Head of Department. He is assisted by two Deputy General Managers and Financial Adviser and Chief Accounts Officer in the discharge of his duties. The Government of India has constituted a Management Committee with the powers of Department of Government of India (except for creation of posts, writing off losses and reappropriation of expenditure).

The present Management Committee comprises of Joint Secretary (Dairy Development) as Chairman, Joint Secretary (Finance). General Manager, Mother Dairy representative of consumers and the General Manager, DMS.

Procurement of milk:

Delhi Milk Scheme has been procureing raw/fresh milk from the following sources:-

(a) Pradeshik Cooperative Dairy Federation, Lucknow (UP)

(b) Haryana Dairy Development Co-operative Federation, Chandigarh.

(c) Milk Federation, Punjab.

(d) Rajasthan State Co-operative Dairy Federation Limited, Jaipur.

(e) Bhartiya Khadi & Gramoudhyog Dudh Utpadak sangh, Budana (U.P.)

(f) Kondli Vikas Co-operative Society, Delhi.

(g) Adarsh Dairy Co-operative Society, Delhi.

(h) Rajasthan Sweets & Dugdh Janya Utpadak Sehakari Samity Ltd., Bikaner.

(i) Delhi State Milk Marketing and Supply Federation.

Production and distribution of milk:

DMS is processing and supplying toned milk containing 3.0% fat and 8.5% SNF and double toned milk containing 1.5% fat and 9% SNF to a network of 1237 outlets spread all over the city. These outlets (milk booths) are manned by students engaged as senior Depot Agents or/Depot Agents and ex-Service Men/Retired Govt./Semi. Govt, Servants as concessionaires.

The DMS is selling toned milk at a rate of Rs. 7 per litre w.e.f. 1.9.1992 and double toned milk at a rate of Rs. 6 per litre. DMS is also supplying milk to 159 institutions such as Hospitals, Govt. Canteens, Schools and Hostels.

The sale price of milk for sale to Govt. Institutions has been revised to Rs. 10.50 per litre with effect from 7.12.1997.

Presently 4.0 lakh litres of milk is sold on an average per day by the DMS-

Besides DMS is also manufacturing and selling ghee and table butter out of surplus fats available. During 1998-99 (upto Nov. 98) the sale of these products has been 357.76 MT and 43.16 MT respectively.

Cost of production and loss

The cost of production of toned milk has increased substantially due to increase in price of raw material and fresh milk. As the selling price of DMS milk has not been revised since 1.9.1992, the loss has increased substantially, This is being met a present by providing budgetary support an(assistance. The figures for the various years arc as follows:

Year	Cost of Production (per litre	Selling Price (per litre in rupees)	Losses (in Rs./Crores in rupees)
1994-95	7.82	7.00	8.91
1995-96	11.28	7.00	47.30
1996-97	11.67	7.00	51.35
1997-98	12.37	7.00	59.22
1998-99 (Upto Nov., 98)	12.77	7.00	46.93

Difficulties and constraints:

The sale price of milk fixed by DMS is f, below the market price. As a result, the DMS incurring substantial losses and the capacity utilisation is linked to the amount of budgetary support that can be provided by the Ministry to cover this loss.

Measures under taken to improve effciency

DMS has under taken upgradation/mordcrnisation of the plant and machinery from tin, to time. During the corrent financial year, an outlay, of Rs. I crore (Rs. 50 lakhs for purchase replacement of plant and equipment and Rs. 50 lakhs for civil works) has been provided. Out of this Rs. 50-21 lakhs has been utilised. Civil works have be sanctioned and the entire amount is likely to I utilised before the end of the current financial year

Quality control Standards have been made stringent to ensure supply of high quality milk. Iinstant sodium meter has been included in the equipment installed in Quality Control Laboratory for rapid assessment of neutralisers added to m and milk products.

A complaint Cell has been setup. It works round the clock with the objective of attending complaints within 48 hours. To overcome the traffic congestion light commercial vehicles have been introduced during i year.

Bonus to employees:

Productivity linked bonus for the year 19, 98 equivalent to 40 days wages have been paid.

New primary dairy cooperatives:

The scheme aims to establish 25.000 new village dairy cooperative societies in the Operation

Flood districts. Under the scheme grants will be provided for the establishment of dairy cooperative societies. The objectives of the Scheme are (a) bring more farmers under cooperative fold (b) full utilisation of processing and chilling capacities already built up. The scheme is yet to be approved by the appraisal agencies. 4.22 Vidya Dairy:

The scheme has been proposed for providing financial assistance to Dairy Science Colleges/Universities to establish a viable dairy plant for improvement in the standards of the trainee. From the view of viability, the capacity of such plant, will vary from place to place and a plant with a processing capacity between 10,000 to 50,000 Hires per day can be viable depending upon the availability of milk, strength of the college, support from the Union and market demand. The Scheme is yet to be approved by the appraisal agencies, including the Planning Commission.

7

Fisheries

Fisheries sector occupies a very important place in the socio-economic development of the country. It has been rccognised as a powerful income and employment generator as it stimulates growth of a number of subsidiary industries, and is a source of cheap and nutritious food besides being a foreign exchange carrier. Most importantly, it is tile source of livelihood for a large section of economically backward population of the country.

The challenges facing fisheries development in the country have been an assessment of fishery resources and their potential in terms of fish production, development of sustainable technologies for fin and shelf fish culture, yield optimisation, and harvest-post harvest operations. The strengthening of infrastructure for production of fish seed, berthing and landing facilities for fishing vessels, as well as welfare of fishermen arc equally important priorities of this sector.

Thrust areas

Fisheries is a State subject and as such the primary responsibility for development rests with State Governments. The major thrust in fisheries development has been focussed oil optimizing production and productivity, augmenting export of marine products, generating employment and improving the welfare of fishermen and their socioeconomic status.

Highlights

— The production of fish reached tile targeted level of 53.9 lakh tonnes in 1997-98. A record production of 56.0 lakh tonnes of fish is anticipated in 1998-99.

— The network of 422 Fish Farmers' Development Agencies (FFDAs) continue to provide technical, financial and extension support to fish farmers. An area of 4.56 lakh ha has been brought under intensive fish culture and 8.30 lakh fish farmers have been benefited by FFDAs up to 1997-98. Tile agencies have also trained 5.77 lakh fish farmers in improved practices.

— Fish seed production of 15904 million fry has been achieved during 1997-98.

— The 39 Brackishwater Fish Farmers' Development Agencies (BFDAs) functioning in tile country have developed an area of about 733 ha. during 1997-98, and 326 shrimp farmers have been trained by them.

— Six major fishing harbours, 29 minor fishing harbours and 125 fish landing centres have been commissioned so far for providing landing and berthing facilities. During 1997-98, ten fish landing centres have been sanctioned at a total cost of Rs. 1259.00 lakhs, and five fish landing centres have been commissioned.

— Increased allocations have been provided for development of model fishermen villages, group accident insurance, and saving cum relief schemes for the welfare of fishermen.

For achieving accelerated growth and enhancing production and productivity of fish and marine products, the Department is implementing 15 plan schemes in this sector, These also include two schemes, viz. Fishery Survey of India and Assistance to Coast Guard which were transferred from the Ministry of Food Processing Industries. The progress and achievements made under various schemes during 1998-99 are stated in subsequent paragraphs.

Development of freshwater aquaculture

Development of freshwater aquaculture is one of tile most important production oriented programmes implemented by the states as a centrally sponsored scheme through the Fish Farmers' Development Agencies (FFDAs).

A network of 422 FFDAs has been sanctioned for establishment under this programme covering all tile potential districts in the country. These agencies provide a package of technical, financial and extension support to fish farmers. In order to boost inland fish production, assistance in the form of subsidy is given to fish farmers for construction of new ponds., reclamation/renovation of ponds and tanks., inputs for first year fish culture, running water fish culture, integrated fish farming, fish seed hatchery, fish feed mills, etc. Assistance is also given to progressive fish farmers for purchase of aerators. Subsidy for tile above mentioned activities is given at double the rates to fishermen of scheduled tribes.

Total water area brought under intensive fish culture is about 4.56 lakh hectares upto 1997-98. Government agencies have trained 5.77 lakh fish farmers/fishermen in improved practices. The total number of beneficiaries covered under the programme is about 8.30 lakhs. A one-time grant of Rs. 5.00 lakh for establishment of a training centre for fish farmers is also given to State Govts.

Through assistance to FFDAs, about 30,000 hectares water area is expected to be brought under scientific fish culture during 1998-99. Approximately 35,000 fish farmers are to be trained in improved practices by Govt. agencies during the year. There is a Budget Estimate provision of Rs. 1850 lakh for the year 1998-99 under the FFDA programme. This scheme is proposed to be revised, raising the subsidy component and inclusion of more activities during the Ninth Plan Period.

Fish seed production

Fish seed production during 1997-98 was 15,904 million fry. The production of shrimp seed is about 1000 million per year at present.

Development of Inland fisheries statistics

The programme which was introduced with the intention of evolving a standardised methodology for upgradation of inland fisheries statistics, is being continued during 1998-99. The resource assessment survey work and catch assessment survey work have been completed in 158 and 56 districts respectively under this scheme so far.

Development of brackishwater aquaculture

Development of brackishwater areas for shrimp farming under an area development concept was implemented as a centrally sponsored scheme called "Integrated Brackishwater Fish Farm Development". Currently, the emphasis is on the following components:

(i) Provision of assistance to different categories of small-scale shrimp farmers for establishment of shrimp farms and shrimp seed hatcheries;

(ii) Establishment of demonstration-cum-training centres for imparting training to shrimp farmers;

(iii) Introduction of training components under BFDA programme for imparting training to small-scale shrimp farmers.

This scheme is being revised raising the subsidy portion and with the inclusion of more components during the Ninth Plan and will be renamed as Integrated Coastal Aquaculture.

The main objective of this Centrally sponsored Scheme is to utilise the country's vast brackishwater resources for fish-shrimp culture. Other subsidiary objectives are to increase foreign exchange earnings through increased shrimp production, generation of adequate employment opportunities and increase of income of farmers in coastal areas.

With a view to provide technical, financial and extension support to shrimp farmers in the small-scale sector, 39 Brackishwater Fish Farmers Development Agencies (BFDAs) have been sanctioned in all the maritime states and the UT of A & N Islands. During 1997-98, 326 shrimp farmers were trained benefitting about 226 families dependent upon them. An area of about 733 ha. was developed by 39 BFDAs in the country. The performance of BFDAs was tardy due to the judgement given by Supreme Court in its order dated 11.12.1996 prohibiting non-traditional shrimp culture within the Coastal Regulation Zone i.e. 500 metres from the high tide line. The matter is currently sub-judice.

Shrimp and fish culture project

A Shrimp and Fish Culture Project with World Bank assistance for developing about 3810 ha. of brackishwater area "and about 51,000 ha. of reservoirs/ox-bow lakes in the States of Andhra Pradesh, Bihar, Orissa, Uttar Pradesh and West Bengal became credit-effective from 28th May, 1992. The cost of the Project was originally estimated at about Rs. 283.63 crore (equivalent to US $ 95 million) from 1992-93 onwards for a duration of seven years. About 90% of the total estimated cost or about US $ 85 million will be available as IDA loan assistance.

Later, due to restructuring, the cost of the Project was revised to Rs. 172.66 crores for the development of 797.53 ha. of brackishwater and 68700 ha. of reservoirs & oxbow lakes.

Out of six sites to be developed under the shrimp culture component, Digha and Canning in West Bengal and Banapada cluster of the Jagatiore Banapada site in Orissa were developed to be stocked in June, 1998. At other sites in West Bengal 85% & 95% works have been completed at Dadanpatra and Dighirpar respectively. Under fish culture component, 91 reservoirs and 11 oxbow lakes have been developed.

Programme for training/study tours abroad for officers involved in implementation of the project has been completed. A total number of 83 officers have completed their training/study tour abroad and 5.11 91 BFDA/FFDA extension officers have completed engine their training at the Central Institute of Brackish of Rs water Aquaculture (CIBA), Chennai and the Central which Institute of Freshwater aquaculture, Bangalore.

In Andhra Pradesh, the State Remote Sensing Application Centre was entrusted to undertake the preparation of Enviornmental Management Plans (EMPs) for the State. For Orissa and West Bengal, the work has been assigned to CIBA. The EMP works for Bihar and Uttar Pradesh have been entrusted to Central Inland Capture Fisheries Research Institute, Barrackpore.

The World Bank has lifted the suspension of the credit for the Project imposed by them in January, 1997 following fulfilment of all the action points by the Central Project Unit (CPU) and the Project States.

Strengthening of infrastructure for inland fish marketing

The Centrally Sponsored Scheme on 'Strengthening of infrastructure for Inland Fish Marketing' is being continued during 1998-99. The objective of the scheme is to create facilities for providing remunerative prices to fish farmers and making available fresh fish at reasonable price to consumers. Assistance is also being provided to state Governments for strengthening infrastructural facilities in the shape of fish handling sheds, ice plants, cold storages, insulated/refrigerated transport vans, three wheelers, fish retail, outlets/ kiosks and bicycles with insulated boxes for retail marketing. A total of 41 marketing units have been sanctioned so far to 19 States with a total cost of Rs. 2475.81. lakhs, Rs. 2241.07 lakh have been released to States so far for this purpose. Five States have completed the projects till date, viz Orissa, Nagaland, Manipur, Mizoram and Haryana.

Assistance to coast guard

The Coast Guard is authorised to monitor fishing by foreign vessels under the MZI act, 1981. The need was felt to strengthen their communication facilities by providing funds for ship to shore direct voice (radio) communication in link with fishing vessels. The link will also help the Coast Guard in ensuring safety of the Indian owned vessels fishing at sea, and in rendering any assistance required. This scheme has been introduced to attain this objective.

Development of marine fisheries

Under the Scheme assistance is provided for the following activities;

Motorisation of traditional craft

Under this scheme. 50% of the cost of engine is provided as subsidy (subject to a maximum of Rs. 10,000/- for OBM and Rs. 12,000/- for IBM) which is equally shared by the Centre and the States. Besides, a sum of Rs. 6,000/ - is also provided as grant to fishermen for purchase of gear. In the case of UTs, the entire cost of subsidy on engine and gear is met by the Centre. During 1997-98, 1400 crafts were sanctioned to be motorised with a central subsidy of Rs. 71.45 lakhs. During 1998-99 it is proposed to motorise 3000 crafts.

Reimbursement of central excise duty on HSD oil supplied to mechanised fishing vessels below 20M

The cost of central excise duty on HSD oil Rs. 351.75 per KL is fully subsidised under this scheme, and is borne on a 80:20 basis between the Centre and the States and it is met fully by the Centre in the case of UTs. About Rs. 1100 lakhs was released under the scheme during 1997-98 towards central share of reimbursement cost to benefit about 20,000 small mechanised fishing vessels of less than %20 M. This benefits is being extended to small mechanised fishing vessels during 1998-99.

Enforcement of marine fishing regulation act and setting up of artificial reefs, etc

Under the scheme 100% central grant-in-aid is provided towards the capital cost of procurement of patrol boats in order to carry out surveillance in territorial waters to safeguard the interest of traditional fishermen and to conserve the fishery resources.

A sum of Rs. 1975 lakhs was released under the scheme toward-, partial payment for construction of patrol boats to various States. 26 patrol boats have been sanctioned to various States up to 1997-98. Although the scheme was discontinued beyond Eighth Five Year Plan. It is proposed to provide Rs. 100 lakhs towards the balance of Central commitment under the scheme during 1998-99.

Fishing harbour facilities at major and minor ports

Fishing harbours; are being developed at both major and minor ports, in addition to fish landing centres. The objective of this scheme is to assist in providing appropriate and adequate infrastructure facilities viz breakwaters, wharf, jetty, dredging, reclamation, auction halls, slipway, workshop and navigation facilities for efficient operation of a large number of fishing vessels.

Under this Scheme 100% grant is provided to Port Trusts for construction of fishing harbours at major ports and 50% share is provided to maritime State Governments for construction of minor fishing harbours and landing centres. Union Territories are Provided with 100% grant under the scheme. Since inception and till the end of 1997-98, Government of India have sanctioned 6 major fishing harbours, '45 minor fishing harbours and 153 fish landing centres. Out of these, 6 major fishing harbours, 29 minor fishing harbours and 125 fish landing centres have been completed by the end of 1997-98.

During the year 1997-98, 4 minor fishing harbours at a total cost of Rs. 1259 lakh and 10 fish landing centres were sanctioned at total of Rs. 556.59 lakhs and 5 fish landing centres have been completed.

Welfare programmes for fishermen

The Scheme, has three components:

(i) Development of Model Fishermen villages

(ii) Group Accident Insurance Scheme for Active Fishermen

(iii) Saving-cum-Relief for Marine Fishermen

Development of model fishermen villages

The objective of this component is to provide basic civic amenities such as housing, drinking water and construction of community halls for-fishermen villages. In each village with 10 to 100 housing units, upto 5 tubewells and 1 community hall can be constructed. The expenditure is shared on a 50:50 basis between the Centre and the State Governments. In case of UTs, the entire expenditure is borne by the Centre. During 1997-98, construction of 4561 houses was approved and Rs. 542.88 lakhs were released to various State Governments/UT Administrations for this purpose. It is proposed to sanction 2500 more houses during 1998-99 for which a budget provision of Rs. 513.40 lakhs has been provided.

Group accident insurance scheme for active fishermen

The objective of this component is to provide insurance cover to fishermen actively engaged in fishing. Active fishermen are insured for Rs. 35,000 for one year against death or permanent disability and Rs.17,500 for partial disability. The insurance premium is Rs.12.00 per beneficiary per year. 50 per cent of the premium is subsidised by the Central Government and the remaining 50 per cent is subsidised by the State Government. In case of Union Territories, 100 per cent of the premium is borne by the Govt. of India. A single policy has been taken in respect of all those States/UTs who are participating through FISHCOPFED.

During 1997-98, 11.37 lakh active fishermen were insured and an amount of Rs.71.34 lakhs was released to the State/U.Ts. During 1998-99, it is proposed to cover 11.75 lakh active fishermen under this scheme with a budget provision of Rs. 70.50 lakhs.

Saving-cum-relief for marine fishermen

The objective of this component is to provide financial assistance to fishermen during the lean fishing season. Under this component, beneficiary fishermen contribute a part of their earning during non-lean months @ Rs. 45/- per month. This contribution is matched with equal contribution from Central and State Governments and the tripled amount is distributed back to fishermen in four equal instalments @ Rs. 270/-per month. In case of UTs, their share is also borne by the Central Government. During 1997-98, about 2.23 lakh fishermen were covered under this component, and an amount of Rs. 892.59 lakhs was released as Central assistance to various maritime States/U.Ts. It is proposed to provide an outlay of Rs. 939.60 lakhs in 1998-99 for covering about 2.75 lakh beneficiaries from maritime States/Union Territories.

Fisheries training and extension

The main objective of the scheme is to provide training to fishery personnel so as to assist them in undertaking fisheries extension programmes effectively. The scheme also provides assistance to fisherfolk in upgrading their skills.

To enhance training facilities, the scheme also provides assistance for setting up/upgradation of two training centres in States/UTs. Other components of the scheme are:

(i) To publish short, concise and useful manuals with a view to provide adequate extension material to trainees and personnel associated with fish production and allied activities.

(ii) Production of video films on technologies developed by Research Institutes/Organisations as well as by State Fisheries Departments for the development of fisheries and its publicity through electronic media.

(iii) To conduct meetings/workshops/seminars, etc. which are of national importance and relevant to the fisheries sector.

During 1997-98, an amount of Rs.65.26 lakh was released to various States/Organisations for training of 2009 fish farmers, setting up/upgradation of 5 training centres, preparation of 15 extension manuals, conducting study production of documentary films and organisation of 6 workshops and seminars.

Central fisheries institutes

Central institute of fisheries nautical and engineering training (CIFNET), Kochi

The primary objective of the Institute is to make available sufficient number of trained operatives for fishing vessels and technicians for shore establishments. In addition to the main campus at Kochi, the Institute has units at Chennai and Visakhapatnam. The Institute has total intake capacity of 200 trainees for the two main courses of Mate Fishing vessels Course and Engine driver Fishing Vessels Course which arc of 18 months' duration. During 1997-98, about 193 trainees were trained in these two main training courses. In addition, the Institute also conducts short-term training programmes for sponsored/ depart mental candidates in fishing technology, gear technology, etc. and about 176 candidates were trained in these short-term courses.

Integrated fisheries project (IFP), Kochi

This Project envisages processing, popularization and test marketing of unconventional varieties of fish. The Project has a fleet of five vessels of different sizes, a well-equiped marine workshop and a slipway to slip vessels upto 250 tonnes, an ice-cum-freezing plant, a modern processing unit. It also provides institutional training in various courses. Besides the Head Quarters at Kochi, the Project also has a centre at Visakhapatnam. During 1998-99 about 400 tonnes of fish are expected to be processed and marketed.

Central institute of coastal engineering for fishery (CICEF), Bangalore

5.23.1 The objective of this Institute set up in 1968 is to conduct techno-economic feasibility studies for development of fishing harbours and brackishwater farms.

The Institute situated at Bangalore has been carrying on the following functions'.

(i) Carrying on reconnaissance survey, identify the suitability of sites for fishing harbours.

(ii) Preparation of preliminary construction plans and detailed estimate.

(iii) Conducting engineering and economic investigations.

(iv) Preparation of project feasibility reports for brackishwater shrimp farms.

(v) Designing of shrimp hactchcries and training of personnel.

During 1997-98 the Institute has conducted technical investigations and prepared the project reports for fishery harbours at Okha in Gujarat, Karaikal in Pondicherry, Rameshwaram in Tamil Nadu and also monitored the World Bank Assistance Shrimp culture Project.

Fishery survey of India

The Fishery Survey of India (FSI), is responsible for survey and assessment of marine fi shery resources of the Indian EEZ. With its headquarters at Mumbai, the Institute has seven operational bases at Porbandar, Mumbai, Mormugao and Kochi along the West Coast, Chennai and Visakhapatnam along the east coast and Port Blair in the Andaman & Nicobar Islands.

A total of 12 ocean going survey vessels are being deployed for fisheries resources survey and monitoring. Apart from collection of data for stock assessment studies, the vessels were- also engaged in experimental projects and collection of sea truth data for remote sensing.

8

Plan Schemes, Special Component Plan & Tribal Sub Plan

Plan schemes

Agricultural development is crucial to India's overall progress and this can be achieved by intensifying the agricultural and allied activities as well as by diversification and commercialization of agriculture. A strong and effective food processing sector plays a significant role in diversification of agricultural activities, improving value addition of agricultural produce, increasing employment opportunities and creating surplus for export of agro-food products. This would, however, require policies and plans for improvement of food processing infrastructure including upgradation of technology and enforcement of quality standards, activating domestic market with focus on exports. Taking this into account, the 9th Five Year Plan has been formulated with special emphasis on the following:

i. Creation of infrastructure including cold chain infrastructure

ii. Quality Upgradation and quality control

iii. Research & development

iv. Special incentives for the North-Eastern States, Jammu and Kashmir, hilly areas, backward areas' including tribal areas.

The Ministry of Food Processing Industries has been operating several plan schemes for the development of processed food industry since the inception of 8th plan period. Taking into account the recommendations of the Working Group of Planning Commission, the constraints faced by the industry, the need to accelerate growth of the sector and the priority status accorded to food processing industry by Government, the Ministry of Food Processing Industries is operating the following plan schemes during the 9th Plan:

Scheme for development of infrastructural facilities

The main objectives of the scheme is to:

i) Establish post-harvest infrastructure and cold chain facilities for food processing as well as integrated projects of mushroomshops, gherkins and baby corn.

ii) Establish food processing industrial estates/food parks.

iii) Createinfrastructural facilities for preservation and processing of fish.

Scheme for setting tip/expansion/modernization of food processing industries

The main objective of the scheme is

i) Setting up/expansion/modernization of food processing units.

ii) Modernization of pulse milling units—The objective of this scheme is installation of dryers and dust control systems for drying of pulses & control of dust during processing for increasing productivity and efficiency.

iii) Setting up of mobile fruit & vegetable processing units - The objective of this scheme is propagation of the concept of mobile fruit and vegetable processing facilities which takes the facility of processing to the doorsteps of the farmers.

iv) Dissemination of low cost preservation technology - The objective of this scheme is to -encourage setting up units using low cost preservation technology.

Scheme for development/modernization of meat processing

The objective of the scheme is development of meat processing industries to achieve good quality, hygienic production of meat and meat products, and development/propagation of international quality standards through modernization of abattoirs, adoption of HACCPA & ISO standards, and evolving an effective quality assurance system.

Scheme for development of poultry & egg processing

The objective of the scheme is development of processed poultry and egg products for both domestic and export markets, with assured quality and health standards and also for effecting necessary technological improvement of processing units.

Scheme for research and development

1. Undertake specific R&D Projects on/relating to:

   i. Processing of cereals, pulses, coarse grains and millets and also for improving traditional/ regional foods made from them.

   ii. Study of prevailing post-harvest technology of millets like ragi, jowar and bajra and devise improvements thereto.

   iii. Development of processing technology for the production of intermediate and finished food products including design and building -of prototype equipment/pilot plants.

iv. Fortification of cereals/cereal products for enhancing the nutritional level of our population, especially women and children.

V. Traditional foods of various regions of the country; and

vi. Utilization of by-products of primary food processing like paddy husk, germ, paddy-straw, pulse-corn, peri carp brokens etc.

2. Update processing, packing and storage technologies for all major processed food products so that they meet international standards.

3. Standardization of various factors such as bacteriological standards, level of preservatives, additives, pesticide residue etc. of meat and meat products, development of value added products of commercial importance.

4. Take Lip research & development work for traditional milk products and packaging of milk products.

5. Development of value added products Using low value fish, product development, standardization of processing technology for non-conventional marine resources like snails, clams, mussels, oysters, etc.

6. Development of new cost effective packaging for food products based oil traditional foods, common food grains, dairy products etc., for both domestic and export purposes. Development of design of equipment for manufacture of such products, development of new inexpensive packaging techniques and equipments, analysis of existing packaging methods, material processes, quality control norms studies about improvement in the currently used systems, Studies about newer packaging possibilities.

7. Financial assistance Would also be available for Setting Lip of quality control laboratory for all processed foods.

Scheme for personpower development

The scheme has the following six components:-

i) Personpower development in rural areas (Food Processing & Training Centres).

   The objectives of this scheme is development of rural entrepreneurship and transfer of technology for processing of food products by ctilising locally grown raw materials and providing 'hands oil' experience at such product ion-cum-training centres, while according priority to persons belonging to SCs/STs/OBCs and women.

ii) Personpower development in grain processing industries of raw materials/finished products, preventive maintenance, sailitation, hygiene and development of organizational and planning abilities.

iii) Training of personpower in meat processing.

   The objective of the scheme is training of persons engaged in traditional meat processing activity, in-service workers and unemployed persons.

iv) Training of traditional fisherpersons for skill upgradation in fish processing.

   The objectives of the scheme is training of persons engaged in fish processing units for upgrading the quality of products and improving hygienic conditions.

v) Creation of Infrastructural facilities.

   The objective of this scheme is to create infrastructual facilities like library, laboratories, pilot plants etc. for running Degree/diploma Courses and training programmes for food processing.

vi) Training programmes sponsored by MFPI.

The objective of the scheme is to conduct training programmes sponsored by Ministry of food processing in various areas of food processing.

Scheme for strengthening of traditional fish processing technologies and marketing

This scheme aims at propagation of low cost indigenous technologies for drying of fish, which will result in value addition, and provide hygienically dried fish for domestic and export market.

Scheme for utilization of low value fish to make value added products

The objective of this scheme is establishment of units for commercial production of value added products like protein concentrates, fish wafers, fish sausages, fish soup, fish cutlets, fish balls, fish feed etc., using low value fish.

Scheme for setting up of innovative dairy projects

The objective of the scheme is to encourage introduction of innovative dairy items such as whey protein, protein concentrates, extraction of minerals, casein etc., where new technology and higher value addition is involved.

Scheme for development/improvement of marketing, quality control, storage & transport of meat & meat products

The objective of the scheme is to provide deep freezers/refrigerators to retail outlets, marketing complexes for development of meat markets and shopping centres, provision Of insulators, refrigerated/children vans for transportation of meat, and establishment/improvement of quality control laboratories.

Scheme for generic advertisement on processed foods and marketing assistance

The objective of the scheme is to build awareness among consumers about the advantages of processed foods, and their quality assurance mechanism, both through (i) Generic Advertisement and Publicity and (ii) Market Promotion Campaign for new product mix and brand name support.

Scheme for strengthening of backward linkages in food processing industries

The objective of the scheme is to

i) Increase capacity utilization of fruit & vegetable processing units as well as grain and coarse grain, processing units by ensuring regular supply of raw materials through contract farming;

ii) Ensure remunerative price to farmers by creating direct linkage between farmers and processors; and

iii) Provide high quality seeds/ fertilizers/ pesticides and planting materials to farmers along with technical know-how etc., through the processor.

Scheme for promotion of food processing industries

The objective of the scheme is to :

i) Strengthen the Directorate of Fruit & vegetable Preservation for information, education and quality systems.

ii) Participation in national/international exhibitions/ fairs.

iii) Promotion of studies, surveys etc., in the food processing sector.

iv) Performance awards.

Scheme for strengthening of nodal agencies

The objective of the scheme is to strengthen the designated State Nodal Agencies for food processing by providing financial support for installation of basic office hardware including computer system and internet for collection of detailed field information, preparation of data base, monitoring of assisted projects, coordination of agro food business etc.

Nature of assistance

The assistance under various plan schemes is available to PSUs/Joint Sector/Assisted Sector/NGOs/ Cooperatives and to private entrepreneurs in the form of grant-in-aid and soft loan. However, a higher level of assistance is provided to NGOs/Cooperatives. Special incentives are provided for projects in "difficult areas" like North-Eastern States, Jammu& Kashmir, and Sikkim, island areas and tribal areas.

Special component plan & tribal sub-plan

Tire Schemes formulated by the Ministry are aimed at providing facilities and incentives for promotion of food processing industries in the country. These schemes envisage enhanced scale of assistance for "difficult" areas, including Integrated Tribal Development Project (ITDP) areas. The Schemes from which benefit of plan assistance may accrue to tribal areas and to SC/ST Communities, are indicated below:

Scheme for development of infrastructural facilities

This scheme -envisages financial assistance In the form of grant to PSUs/joint sector/NGOs and cooperatives to the extent of 50% of the cost of capital equipment and technical civil works up to Rs. 25 lakhs in general areas whereas in the case of difficult areas, assistance will be 75% Lip to Rs.50 lakhs. However, loans to PSUs and joint sector units Would be 50% of the total equity subject to a maximum of Rs. 150 lakhs in general areas and Rs.200 lakhs in difficult areas.

Scheme for setting up/expansion/modernisation of food processing industries

Under this scheme, PSUs are eligible to get loan up to 50% of cost of capital equipment and technical civil works up to Rs.150 lakhs in general areas and Rs.200 lakhs in difficult areas or grant Up to 50% of cost of capital equipment and technical civil works up to Rs.50 lakhs in difficult areas would be available. Alternatively, such joint sector units call get grant up to 25% cost of capital cost of technical civil works up to Rs.25 lakhs in difficult areas. In the case of private/assisted sector, loan Up to 50% and up to Rs.50 lakhs in general areas would be provided whereas in the case of difficult areas, they Would be given up to Rs. 75 lakhs. For NGOs and cooperatives, financial assistance in the form of grant up to Rs.25 lakhs in general areas and 50% up to Rs.50 lakhs in difficult areas is provided.

Scheme for development/modernization of meat processing industries

Under this scheme, NGOs, cooperatives, civic bodies and Government organizations are eligible to get grant up to 50% of cost of capital equipment and technical civil works up to Rs.150 lakhs in general areas and 75% of such Cost up to Rs.100 lakhs in difficult areas. In the case of PSUs and joint sector units, assistance will be in the form of grant of up to 75% of cost of capital equipment and technical civil works up to Rs. 100 lakhs in difficult areas. However, assistance in the form of loan would be limited to 50% of cost of capital equipment and technical civil works up to Rs.150 lakhs in general areas and up to Rs.200 lakhs in difficult areas. In the case of private/ assisted sector, assistance will be in the form of grant Up to 50% cost of capital equipment and technical civil works up to Rs. 50 lakhs in difficult areas. For difficult areas, it will be up to Rs.75 lakhs.

Scheme for development of poultry & egg processing

This scheme envisages financial assistance to NGOs and cooperatives in the form of grant up to 50% of the cost of capital equipment and technical civil works up to Rs.75 lakhs in general areas and 75% of such cost up to Rs. 100 lakhs in difficult areas. PSUs and joint sector units are entitled to grant up to 75% of cost of capital equipment and technical civil works up to Rs. 100 lakhs in difficult areas. Assistance in the form of loan Would however be limited to 50% of cost of capital equipments and technical civil works up to Rs.150 lakhs in general areas and up to Rs.200 lakhs in difficult areas. Private and assisted sector units would be eligible to get loan up to 50% of the cost of capital equipments and technical civil works up to Rs.50 lakhs for general areas however in difficult areas, it will be up to, Rs.75 lakhs.

Scheme for strengthening of traditional fish processing and marketing

This scheme envisages financial assistance in the form of grant to NGOs/Cooperatives/joint/assisted/private sector/PSUs up to 50% of the capital Cost up to Rs.10 lakhs in general areas and 75% of the capital cost up to Rs.10 lakhs in difficult areas.

Scheme for Utilisation of Low Value Fish

This scheme envisages financial assistance in the form of grant to NGOs/Cooperatives Up to 50% of the capital cost up to Rs. 10 lakhs in general areas and 75% of the capital cost up to Rs. 10 lakhs in difficult areas.

Though the main Concept Of Our scheme is based Oil project approach, yet about 20% of our plan funds may get apportioned to the schemes benefiting SC/ST Communities.

9

Promotion of Food Processing

Promotion of food processing industries

The Ministry provides assistance for setting up, expansion and modernisation of food processing units including modernisation of pulse milling units.

Fruit & vegetable processing

During the period under review the Ministry provided loan of Rs.20 lakhs to M/s. Aaren Food Private Ltd., Bhubaneshwar for setting up of a unit at Kantabada In Kliurda District in the State of Orissa for manufacture of processed fruits and vegetables.

The Ministry provided financial assistance of Rs.8.51 lakhs to People Action For Rural Development Association (PARDA) for setting up of fruit & vegetable processing unit at Kachi Village in Ukhrul District of Manipur. The Ministry provided a grant of Rs.] 1.2 lakh to Malom Tuliyaima Development Association, Manipur for setting up of a fruit and vegetable processing unit in Bishnupur District.

An assistance of Rs. 10.7 lakh was provided to Rural Areas Development Association, (RADA), Manipur for setting up of bamboo shoot processing plant at New Lukhambi in Tamenglong district.

Pork processing

Ministry approved an assistance of Rs.298 lakhs to State

Federation of Piggery Farmers, Nagaland for establishment of Integrated Pork Processing Project in Medzifema, Dimapur. Out of this assistance of Rs. 99 lakhs was provided during the period under review. The unit is under construction.

The Assam Livestock and Poultry Corporation was also approved a grant of Rs. 175 lakhs for establishment of an Integrated Pork Processing Project at Nazira. The project is in the final stages of implementation.

In the state of Orissa, a project on Integrated Pork Processing was sanctioned and grant-in-aid of Rs.100 lakhs has been approved. Out of this, an assistance of Rs.33 lakhs has been provided during the period under review.

The Ministry has approved a grant-in-aid of Rs. 65 lakhs to MAFCO, Koregaon, Maharashtra for modernisation of meat processing plant. Out of this amount, Rs.32.5 lakhs has been released during the Current year.

Cereal based products

An amount of Rs. 25 Lakhs has been provided to Messrs. North Lakhimpur Food Processors Pvt. Ltd. Co., North Lakhimpur, Assam as grant for setting up of a biscuit manufacturing unit.

Development of infrastructure facility

Development of food processing infrastructure is essential for growth of a strong food processing sector. The Ministry provides financial assistance for establishment of post-harvest infrastructure and cold chain facilities and food processing and for integrated projects of mushrooms, hops, gherkins, etc., setting up of food processing industrial estates and food parks; and infrastructure facilities for preservation and processing of fish. Establishment and strengthening of post harvest infrastructure helps in reducing wastage of agriculture raw material and ensures availability of agro products throughout the year for the processing unit as well as for direct consumption.

During the year under review Ministry provided a grant of Rs.14.97 lakhs to M/s. Vandaninadu Development Society, Kerala (Non- Government Organisation) for setting up of a spawn lab at Idukki in the State of Kerala.

During the year M/s. Khamderaya Grape Growers Cooperative Society have been provided a grant of Rs. 15.22 lakhs for setting LIP of a cold storage at Sangli in the State of Maharashtra.

M/s. Khyati Cold Storage Limited have been provided a loan of Rs.25 lakhs during the year for setting up of a cold storage in the State of Gujarat.

10

Promotional Support

Under the plan scheme for "Promotion of Food Processing Industries", the Ministry provides assistance to Government Departments, Government Undertakings/ Organ i sat ions, Non-Government Organisations and Industry Associations for organising exhibitions, workshops, seminars, conferences, symposium with the objective of dissemination of information regarding food processing industries, familiarizing the existing and prospective entrepreneurs with modern techniques of production and packaging, development of market and popularization of products,. It also provides assistance for undertaking studies and surveys for assessment of potential for food processing industries on sectoral and regional basis.

The scheme also envisages financial assistance for Entrepreneurial Development Programmes (EDP). During the year 1998-99, following major exhibitions, workshops, seminars, conferences, studies, entrepreneurial development programmes have been sponsored/assisted by this Ministry.

Exhibitions

The Ministry of Food Processing Industries sponsored the international exposition "Agro-Advantage Maharashtra '98" organised by Government of Maharashtra, during

November 6-9, 98 at Mumbai, to attract investment in the food processing sector.

The exposition was a show-window 'for display of the latest technology in the field of agro food sector from all over the world. The Ministry of Food Processing Industries took active part in the exposition. Secretary (FPI) and other senior officers of the Ministry also participated in the convention, which attracted over 800 delegates. On this occasion, definitive interests have been shown by many national and international groups for investment, in food processing projects with investment outlay exceeding Rs.2000 crores. The Government of Maharashtra will be taking follow up action in this regard.

The Ministry sponsored the International Food Convention (IFCON'98) organised by Association of Food Scientists and Technologists (India), at CFTRI, Mysore during November 24-27, 199 8 to bring on a common platform the captains of food industry, research scientists and technologists from universities and premier research institutions and other food professionals to debate and deliberate upon the emerging issues confronting the country in the face of liberalisation and globalisation of market economies. Secretary (FPI) and other senior officers of the Ministry also attended the convention. Secretary (FPI) presided over the inauguration & opening of Food Expo' 98. He also made a presentation on "Globalisation of Indian Food Industry -Problems & Perspective". The event was attended by a large number of national and international scientists and technologists.

The Ministry of Food Processing Industries participated in the exhibition "Agro-Tech' 98" organised by the Confederation of Indian Industry, Northern Region, at Chandigarh from December 2-6, 1998. The exhibition provided opportunities for interaction and transaction of business to visitors including high power delegation from SAARC nations. Secretary (FPI) and other senior officers of the Ministry also attended the exhibition. Secretary (FPI) inaugurated the International Conference on Fruit & Vegetable Processing which was held on December 2, 1998. This Ministry provided financial assistance for the event.

The Bengal Chamber of Commerce & Industry Guwahati Chapter, organised an exhibition and a seminar "Expo-North East' 98" at Guwahati from 515 December, 1998. NERAMAC, a public sector undertaking under the administrative control of this Ministry, participated in the above event on behalf of the Ministry. The Ministry provided financial assistance for holding this exhibition and seminar on food processing.

The Ministry of Food Processing Industries participated in an exhibition on India's Vision for Future and Achievements of the past 50 years, organised at National Stadium, New Delhi from 5-15th August, 1998. A 30 minute audio visual display, highlighting India's achievements in science and technology over the last 50 years was also shown in the Central Hall of the Parliament House on 15th August, 1998 by the Department of Science & Technology.

The Ministry of Food Processing Industries participated in the Industrial Exhibition organised by Indian Industries Association, which is the APEX body of Small Industries in the State of Uttar Pradesh, at Muzaffarnagar from 4-5th October 1998 exhibition was inaugurated by Shri Sompal, Minister of State for Agriculture.

Seminars & workshops

The Ministry assisted the Centre for Processed Food, Bangalore in organising an international seminar on

'Modified Atmosphere Packaging & Controlled Atmosphere Storage, during April 27-28, 1998 at Bangalore.

This Ministry participated in a "workshop on Packaging of Wheat Flours" organised by the Roller Flour Mills Federation of India at New Delhi on June 19, 1998 to help the manufacturers to improve the packaging methods and explore world market for their products. The workshop was inaugurated by Secretary (FPI).

The World Association for Small & Medium Enterprises, New Delhi in collaboration with National Research Development Corporation organised the Asia-China Technology & Economic Cooperation Expo' 98 (SATAX'98) at New Delhi from 27-30 July, 1998 to promote technological trade & economic cooperation between India and other countries in South Asian Region in FPI & other selected industrial sector. Secretary (FPI) delivered a key note address at the convention. The Ministry also provided financial assistance to the event.

A national seminar on Problems of Small & Marginal Farmers in Marketing of Fruits and Vegetables was organised by the Farmers Education & Welfare Society at New Delhi on the 20th & 21st August 1998. The Ministry provided assistance for holding of this seminar.

The Ministry sponsored a national conference on " The Future of Processed Fruit And Vegetable Industry - Summit '98" hosted by the India Export & Economic Foundation in coordination with All India Food Preservers' Association at Bangalore on August 21-22, 1998. The objective of the conference was dissemination of information amongst the exporters, entrepreneurs, consultants, technologists, statutory authorities and policy makers to build a strong interface between agriculture and industry and to highlight the problems and prospects of exporting processed fruits and vegetables.

ILSI-INDIA, New Delhi, organised a workshop on Science Based Approaches to Harmonisation of Regulatory Food Quality and Safety Measures in SAARC Region to provide scientific inputs for harmonisation of food regulations within member countries of SAARC. The Workshop was inaugurated by Secretary (FPI).

The Department of Business Economics, University of Delhi organised an industrial seminar on 27 October 1998 to promote the study of food processing industries in India in regard to technology, marketing and supply chains, foreign participation etc.

The Ministry provided assistance to Confederation of Indian Food Trade & Industry, New Delhi to organise "Food Processing Summit '98" on 14th November 1998 at New Delhi on "Challenges of Globalisation, Time for Introspection". The seminar was inaugurated by Secretary (FPI).

A one-day seminar on "Potential of Food Processing Industries in North-East with Special reference to Tripura" was held on 16th November 1998 in Agartala. The seminar was organised by the Government of Tripura at the initiative of this Ministry. It was inaugurated by the Chief Minister of Tripura and was attended by Ministers of the Government of Tripura, Members of Parliament, Secretary (FPI) and other senior officers of this Ministry besides representatives of CFTRI, NERAMAC and a large number of entrepreneurs. The seminar was very useful in highlighting the potential of food processing industries in Tripura. Financial assistance was provided for organisation of the seminar.

ILSI-INDIA and Micro-nutrient Initiative, South

Asian Regional Offices have organised a national conference on 'Micro-nutrient Fortification of Food' at Jaipur from 8-9 Feb. '99 against the background of high incidence of malnutrition in the country particularly resulting from vitamin A, iodine and iron deficiencies.

The conference was attended by experts from India and abroad to discuss important issues relating to micro-nutrient fortification of food and safety, regulatory & educational advocacy aspects of food fortification programme in India.

The National Productivity Council, New Delhi is organised a national seminar on "Quality for Leadership-challenges for Indian Food Industry" during February, 1999. The proposed seminar will be very useful for food processing industries in India. This Ministry sponsored this seminar.

Studies

This Ministry has entrusted the National Research Development Corporation to conduct a preferability study for setting Lip an Integrated coconut processing complex in Andaman & Nicobar Islands at a cost of Rs.5.00 lakhs. This Ministry has taken initiative to develop coconut processing facilities in these Islands.

The Ministry of Food Processing Industries has given, in principle, approval to support APEDA's proposal to undertake a techno-feasibility study on cold chain linkages in three States. This study is being done by ATO-DLO, a research organisation under the Ministry of Agriculture, Government of Netherlands. The techno-feasibility exercise in respective states will evolve a strategy for designing a supply chain grid leading to a pilot project for a few specific commodities for ensuring reduction in post-harvest losses and wastage. The study would be an attempt to strike a balance between supply, distribution, storage and demand. The financial implications are being worked out by APEDA.

The Ministry has sponsored a study by the Northeaster Industrial and Technical Consultancy Organisation Ltd. (NEITCO), Guwahati on Integrated Master Plan for food processing industry in the Northeastern region and also the role of NERAMAC in this context. The study would focus on the strategy for developing the food processing sector in the region after taking into account the availability of raw material, existing infrastructure and consumer demand. This will also bring out the role which needs to be played by North-Eastern Regional Agricultural Marketing Corporation Ltd. (NERAMAC).

Entrepreneurial development programme

Uttar Pradesh Consultants Limited, Kanpur will be organising two Entrepreneurial Development Programmes in Food Processing Industries at Pratapgarh and Allahabad on the subject of Aonwla processing and guava processing respectively. This programme will help in generating self-employment/ entrepreneurship in the State. This Ministry is providing financial assistance for the two events.

Haryana-Delhi Industrial Consultancy Limited, New Delhi will conduct an Entrepreneurial Development Programme in food processing industries in March, 1999 to identify the prospective entrepreneurs as well as potential investment opportunities. The programme will help in setting up of small units by the prospective entrepreneurs. This Ministry is providing financial assistance for this purpose.

Promotional interactions

The Ministry participated in the International Green

Week Fair (IGW) 1998 held in Germany in the month of January 1998. The IGW Fair is a major consumer fair of Europe for food products and is held every year in Germany for the last six decades. The Ministry's participation this time was at a scale larger than that of the previous year, with Agricultural Products Export Development Authority (APEDA) in association with this Ministry having put up a stall for 'all the 10 days of the fair.

A representative of the Ministry participated as a member in the Promotion Mission led by a senior officer of the Ministry of Industry, Department of Industrial Policy & Promotion, which visited France from 20th to 26th September, 1998. This was In connection with a one day event called "Indo-French Investment Forum" being organised by that Ministry in New Delhi to make a sectoral representation to some of the French medium-sized companies followed by one-to-one meetings. Food processing including packaging is one of the thrust areas selected for the event.

Indo-Italian Joint Working Group on Food Processing was constituted in 1998 by the Ministry under the co-chairmanship of Joint Secretary in charge of International Cooperation Division in the Ministry from Indian side and Dr. Pasquale D' Acunzi, President of ANICAV and Vice-President of Federalimentare (Italian Food Federation) from the Italian side. This Ministry, being the nodal Ministry also provides secretariat to the Working Group. The first session of the Working Group was held in Rome on 15th and l6th December, 1998. The two delegations agreed upon various projects for cooperation.

11

R & D Human Resource Development

Research & development

The Ministry gives special emphasis Oil Supporting Research & Development (R&D) activities in tile food processing sector. Efforts have been made to widen the R&D base in food processing by involvement of various R&D institutions and by funding of laboratory/industry projects as well as purely industry projects. The Ministry provides grant for R&D projects specially for development of traditional foods, for product, process and packaging innovations, and utilisation of by products of the primary food production system as well as of the food processing industry.

Paddy processing research centre

The Paddy Processing Research Centre (PPRC) at Thanjavur, an autonomous body under tile administrative control of the Ministry, is carrying out basic research work oil different applied aspects of rice processing and by-products utilisation like drying, storage, parboiling, milling, bran stabilisation and oil extraction, etc. Currently the projects being handled at the Paddy Processing Research Centre (PPRC), Thanjavur are:

(a) Optimization of parameters for curing of rice.

(b) Standardisation of thermic fluid parboiling of brown rice.

(c) The influence of water soluble chlorides on the production of white core parboiled rice.

The activities of PPRC are being expanded in the field of research & development, transfer of technology, training & human resource development, & administration & require technology upgradation and diversification.

Assistance to R&D projects

The Ministry has provided assistance of Rs. 3.22 lakhs to Indian Institute of Technology (IIT) Delhi for undertaking a research project entitled "Development of Process Technology for Hops Extraction". The project is basically aimed at setting up of processing facilities to manufacture value added products from hops i.e. pellets and extracts.

During the year, Ministry provided an assistance of Rs. 2.77 lakhs to Indian Institute of Packaging, Mumbai for undertaking research projects entitled "Packaging of Doodhi Halwa" and "Packaging of Banana Chips". The main objective of the projects is to develop appropriate packaging system for increasing shelf life of the products for appropriate marketing and distribution.

During the period under review, the Ministry provided further assistance of Rs. 1 lakh to Planters Energy Network, Madurai for their ongoing project of survey of the potential food processing industries with hot air requirements, working out present energy consumption and specific energy utilisation process in order to arrive at the potential for utilisation of solar energy.

Human resource development

During the IXth Plan period, the food processing industry is expected to grow rapidly. The demand for trained manpower to man the growing needs of the food processing industry will also become tremendous.

This is more so because the existing food industry will also require technology upgradation and diversification. Besides, for management of quality control systems trained manpower will be essential. While the organised food industry will require formally trained manpower, there will also be need for developing entrepreneurs with certain amount of skill so that they can extend and absorb technologies for upgrading their existing operations. With a view to extend the spread of food processing units in the remote areas closer to the raw material sources, there will be need for developing entrepreneurship in such areas for production, packaging and distribution of processed food products.

Scheme for assistance to HRD institutions

During the year 1998-99, the Ministry launched a Scheme for Person Power Development in food processing industries under which assistance is available to HRD Institutions, As per the scheme, a grant up to Rs. 5 0 lakhs can be given to HRD Institutions such as Colleges, Universities, Technical Institutions, Management Institutions etc. to create infrastructural facilities like libraries, laboratories, etc. for running degree/diploma courses and training programmes for food processing.

Food processing training centres

In order to develop skill and entrepreneurship in fruit and vegetable processing, specially in rural areas, Ministry has provided assistance for setting up 231 food processing training centre in the 8th Plan in almost all the states. As many as 123 such training centres are reported to have already been established and training imparted to almost 6,163 trainees. Some of the trainees are reported to have already established their own processing units in tiny/small scale sector. During the period under review (up to 25.2,1999), similar assistance has also been extended for setting up of 31 food processing training centres in various locations in the country.

Ministry has also sponsored training courses for the workers and professionals of meat industry. About 1400 candidates have been trained in meat and poultry processing in the states of Andhra Pradesh, Assam, Manipur, UP, Mysore, Karnataka and Tamilnadu.

12

Food Safety & Quality

Fruit products order (FPO)

Fruit Products Order - 1955, promulgated under Section 3 of tile Essential Commodities Act - 1955, aims at regulating sanitary and hygienic conditions in manufacture of fruit, vegetable products. It Is mandatory for all manufacturers of fruit & vegetable products to obtain a licence under this Order. To ensure good quality products, manufactured under hygienic conditions, the Fruit Product Order lays down the minimum requirements for:

1. Sanitary and hygienic conditions of premises, surroundings and personnel.
2. Water to be used for processing.
3. Machinery and equipment.
4. Product standards.

Besides this, maximum limits of preservatives, additives and contaminants have also been specified for various products.

This order is implemented by Ministry of Food Processing Industries through the Directorate of Fruit & Vegetable Preservation at New Delhi. The Directorate has four regional offices located at Delhi, Mumbai, Calcutta and Chennai, as well as sub-offices at Lucknow and Guwahati. The officials of the Directorate undertake frequent inspections of the manufacturing units and draw random samples of products from tile manufacturers and markets which are analysed in the laboratories to test their conformity with tile specifications laid under FPO.

The Central Fruit Advisory C..mittee comprising of the officials of concerned Government Departments, technical experts, representatives of

Central Food Technology Research Institute, Bureau of Indian Standards, Fruit and Vegetable Producers and Processing Industry, is responsible for recommending amendments in the Fruit Product Order. In view of the demands of the industry, and the liberalised economic scenario, major amendments were made in FPO during 1997.

Meat food products order (MFPO)

Meat Food Products Order, 1973 (MFPO) promulgated under the provisions of Essential Commodities Act, 1955 provides for sanitary and other requirements, limits of heavy metals, preservatives, insecticides, residue, etc., for meat food products. This Order was being implemented by Department of Rural Development in tile Ministry of Rural Area & Employment. As oil 3 1 st March, 1998 there were 128 licences issued under MFPO 1973. As per the recent amendment to tile Allocation of Business, Ministry of Agriculture (Deptt. of Agriculture & Cooperation) would now be the Administrative Ministry for this Order.

Milk & milk products order (MMPO)

Milk and Milk Products Order, 1992 administered by the Department of Animal Husbandry & Dairying under Ministry of Agriculture was promulgated oil 9th June, 1992 under the provision of Section 3 of the Essential Commodities Act, 1955 with a view to maintain ail increased supply of liquid milk of desired quality to the general public. This Order regulates production, supply and distribution of milk and milk products throughout the country. The Order also seeks to ensure the observance of sanitary requirements for dairies, machinery and premises, and quality control standards for milk and milk products. So far, 254 registration certificates under MMPO, 1992 has been issued by Department of Animal Husbandry and Dairying.

Codex alimentarius

The term Codex Alimentarius is taken from Latin and means food code. Codex. Alimentarius brings together all the interested parties - scientists, technical experts, governments, consumers and industry representatives to help develop standards for food manufacturing and trade. These standards, guidelines and recommendations are recognized worldwide for their vital role in protecting the consumer and facilitating international trade. As Codex Alimentarius represent scientifically and technically based standards that represent a consensus of food and trade experts from around the world, these standards are more and more being used in international trade negotiations and also for settling of disputes by WTO.

The Codex Contact Point in India is the Directorate General of Health Services (DGHS) in the Ministry of Health; however, the Ministry of Food Processing Industries is closely associated with the activities of Codex Alimentarious. Under the Plan schemes, a scheme for setting up of Codex Monitoring Cell in the Ministry with the allocations of Rs.58.00 lakhs in 1998-99 has been formulated for creating data base, technical examination of various standards in association with experts.

A delegation led by a senior officer of this Ministry participated in the meeting of the Codex Committee on Food Labelling at Ottawa from 25th to 29th May, 1998.

Another Officer from this Ministry was Member of the Indian delegation for the meeting of the Codex Committee on General Principles held at Paris, France from 7th to 11th September, 1998.

Food quality

The Ministry cleared a proposal for release of Rs. 5 9.2 lakhs to Food Research and Analysis Centre, New Delhi for upgradation of its Food Analysis and Quality Control Laboratory for analysis of food products. The main objective of the proposal is to upgrade the existing analytical laboratory and bring it on par with any other modem analytical laboratory in the country.

During the year under review, the Ministry cleared a proposal in principle for release of 12.32 lakhs to CCS Haryana Agricultural University, Hissar for upgradation of quality control and food analysis laboratory of the Department of Food Science and Technology of the University. The main objectives of the proposal are to provide quality assurance and analytical services to the food processing industries, to undertake micro biological examination of various pathogen and mycotoxins and to estimate nutritional parameters including minerals, vitamins, food value in calories, protein carbohydrates, fats etc.

Hazard analysis and critical control point (HACCP)

Hazard Analysis and Critical Control Point (HACCP) is an important quality assurance system. This system ensures that the products are safe and of good quality. The system is extremely desirable in view of the changing scenario in the international trade. The Ministry provides grant of 50% subject to a limit of Rs. 10 lakhs towards the cost of implementing Total Quality Management (TQM) including HACCP and ISO-9000 certifications.

This Ministry sponsored a one-day seminar and five day training programme organised by APEDA from 30th November to 5th December 1998 in collaboration with NSF-Intemational strategic Registration Limited'. USA, which is the main authority for certifying HACCP-9000. HACCP is an important requirement for ensuring the quality of products from health and safety aspects and is crucial for exports.

13

Public Sector Enterprise

Modern Food Industries (I) Limited was incorporated in 1965 under the name of Modern Bakeries-(1) Limited. The present name was adopted in November, 1982 in order to reflect its diversified activities.

Capital structure

The authorised share capital of the Company is Rs. 15.00 crores and the paid up capital is Rs. 13.01 crores as oil 3 1.12.1998. The outstanding loans repayable by the Company to the Government of India stood at Rs.5.20 crores as oil 3 1.12.1998 against Rs.14.73 crores oil 3 1.12.1997.

Physical performance

(i) Bread

The Company continued to produce and market different varieties of bread like white sandwich bread, sweet bread, milk bread, fruity bread, brown bread and special bread at its 14 bread manufacturing units located at Ahmedabad, Bangalore, Mumbai, Calcutta, Chandigarh, Cochin, Delhi (2 units), Hyderabad, Indore, Jaipur, Kanpur, Chennai & Ranchi. The total sale of bread during the period April 1998 to December, 1998 was 12. 10 crore standard loaves of 400 gms (SL) as compared to 14.37 crores SL during the corresponding period of last year.

For further growth in production and marketing or bakery products and to provide wholesome and hygienically produced bread at reasonable prices to greater number of Consumers in the country, the company developed the concept of production and marketing of bread through franchises. As oil 3 1.12.1998 the company had 22 operating franchise units in various parts of the country. The company produced and sold 490.20 lakhs SL of breads through franchise arrangements during April to December, 1998. This is over and above company's own sales reported above. This also brought income to the company in the shape of royalty amounting to Rs.47.72 lakhs as compared to a royalty amount Of Rs.40.00 lakhs during the period April to December, 1997.

(i) Energy food

(a) Fruit juice bottling plant, Delhi :

The plant continues to produce and market Rasika Fruit Drinks. The sale of Rasika during April to December, 1998 was 0.52 lakh crates (of 24 bottles of 200 ml each) against 0.76 lakh crates during the corresponding period last year,

During the period April to December, 1998, apart from the bottling activity the unit has also supplied 22264.625 NIT of Energy Food to UP Government for their Social Welfare Programmes as compared to 20137 NIT of Energy Food during the corresponding period of last year. As an alternate item of Energy Food, the unit also supplied 4707.082 NIT of Nutro-Biscuits to UP Government during the above period, as compared to 4490 MT during corresponding period of previous year.

(b) Roller flour mill, Faridabad

During the period April to December, 1998 the unit has Supplied 10638 MT of Energy Food to the States of UP and Bihar under their various nutritional programmes as compared to 11543 NIT supplied during the corresponding period of last year.

(c) Bhagalpur unit

During the period April to December, 1998 this unit has supplied 1558 NIT of Energy Food to Bihar Government under their various Social Welfare Programmes as compared to 2312 NIT supplied during the corresponding period of last year.

(d) Kanpur unit

Besides production of bread, during the period April to December, 1998, this unit has supplied 6893 *NIT* of Energy Food to UP Government for their Social Welfare Programme as compared to 4287 *NIT* supplied during the corresponding period of last year.

(e) Extruder food plant, Jaipur

The unit supplied 2311 NIT of Extruded Food during April to December, 1998 as compared to supply of 2689 *NIT* during the corresponding period of last year to the various Welfare Programmes of the Government of Rajasthan.

Research and development

The company has its own in-house research and development laboratory. This laboratory is recognized by Department of Scientific and Industrial Research, Ministry of Science and Technology, Government of India. The research facilities at this laboratory are used for development of new products for commercial market and also identification and development of certain bread improvers and other ingredients to improve the quality of existing varieties of bread produced by the company.

New projects/activities or their expansion

The company has set up its own production facilities for

manufacture of cakes at Mumbai and the work for another cake plant at Cochin is in progress.

The Company has also taken possession of land and the shed for setting up of Energy Food Plant at Patna.

Financial performance

The company's turnover during April to December, 1998 is Rs. 11972.23 lakhs as compared to Rs. 125 84.47 lakhs in the corresponding period of last year. The turnover was Rs.18151.70 lakhs during 1997-98 as compared to Rs.16682.25 lakhs during 1996-97.

Performance

The company carried a profit of Rs.7.64 crores during 1997-98 as against a profit of Rs. 16.45 crores in 1996-97. However on account of various problems faced by the company during the period April, 1998 to December, 1998 the performance is not satisfactory.

Dividend

The company paid a dividend at the rate of 8.5% of the equity for the year 1997-98 amounting to Rs.97.56 lakhs as against 20% for the year 1996-97.

Physical sales

Physical sales for the period April to December, 1998 vis-a-vis April to December, 1997 and actuals of 1997-98 are as follows:

Disinvestment

The Government has decided to disinvest 74% of its equity in MFIL to a Strategic Partner. M/s ANZ Grindlays Bank Ltd. have been appointed as Global Advisor to advice and assist the Government in the selection of a stregic partner through a global process of Competitive selection.

Staff strength

The details regarding total No. of employees and No. of SC/ST employees and their percentage is given below:-

(in MT)

Category of Employees	Total No.	SC	%age	ST	%age
Category-I	128	12	9.37	01	0.78
Category-II	148	14	9.45	01	0.67
Category-IIIA	1041	142	13.64	27	2.59
Category-IIIB	1101	229	20.79	43	3.90

North eastern regional agricultural marketing cooperation limited (NERAMAC)

North Eastern Regional Agricultural Marketing Corporation Ltd. (NERAMAC), Guwahati was set up in March, 1982 with the main objective of undertaking marketing and processing of fruits and vegetables grown in the North Eastern Region. The authorized share capital of the Corporation is Rs.500 lakhs and the paid-up capital is Rs.369 lakhs.

The Corporation's first major project viz. Pineapple Juice Concentrate Plant set up at Naikata in the State of Tripura was commissioned in June, 1988. The plant produced 75.60 NIT of Pineapple Juice Concentrate (PJC) during the period April, 1998 to December, 1998 as compared to 79.82 MT during the corresponding period of last year.

The Corporation has taken up processing of cashew in a big way. It had produced 11.94 MT of processed cashew during the period April, 1998 to December, 1998 as against 16.59 MT during the corresponding period last year.

The Corporation actively supported the small and tiny producers of processed foods of North-Eastern region and marketed their products.

The Corporation also continued with trading activities and undertook trading of commodities such as minor forest products, fertilizers, honey, etc.

The Corporation's turnover during April 1998 to December, 1998 was Rs.87.49 Lakhs as compared to Rs.85.35 lakhs during the corresponding period of 1997-98.

The Corporation after having turned sick was referred to Board of Industrial Finance and Reconstruction (BIFR). The Government has approved a rehabilitation package of Rs. 10. 3 6 crores which after getting concurrence of BIFR would be immediately implemented. This will facilitate healthy operation of this Corporation to the best advantage of the North Eastern states.

The staff strength position as on 31.12.1998 was 77. The number of Scheduled Castes and Scheduled Tribes as on this date was 13 and 9 respectively.

Number of rice mills as on 1.1.1999

Name of State	Hullers	Shellers Cum Shellers	Huller	Modem/ Modernised Rice Mills	Total
1. Andhra Pradesh	4609	1776	2364	12995	21744
2. Assam	431	14	2133	242	2820
3. Bihar	4749	63	9	51	4872
4. Gujarat	1890	159	67	1045	3161
5. Haryana	807	-	-	990	1797
6. Himachal Pradesh	890	1	3	222	1116

7. Jammu & Kashmir	-	-	-	-	-
8. Karnataka	9131	462	1103	3674	14370
9. Kerala	13664	-	13	2533	16210
10. Madhya Pradesh	3918	201	262	1661	6042
11. Maharashtra	8199	273	541	1759	10772
12. Manipur	838	-	-	560	1398
13. Meghalaya	252		8	-	260
14. Nagaland	-	-	-	-	-
15. Orissa	6398	125	289	552	7364
16. Punjab	4416	442	-	1965	6823
17. Rajasthan	152	2	6	193	353
18. Sikkim	17	-	-	-	7
19. Tamil Nadu	13684	448	1324	3922	19378
20. Tripura	1030	6	8	1	1045
21. Uttar Pradesh	5707	562	150	1215	7634
22. West Bengal	9554	3	72	926	10555
23. Andaman&Nicobar	116	-	-	-	116
24. Arunachal Pradesh	-			-	-
25. Chandigarh	16			11	27
26. Dadra&Nagar Haveli	8	1		-	9
27. Delhi	2	-	-	27	29
28. Goa	670	-	25	56	751
29. Mizoram	-	-	-	-	-
30. Pondicherry	138	-	8	88	234
31. Lakshadweep					
Total	91287	4538	8385	34688	138898

Number of rolled flour mills in the country as on 01-01-1999

S No.	Name of the State	Number
1.	Andhra Pradesh	58
2.	Assam	40
3.	Bihar	58
4.	Chandigarh	5
5.	Delhi	18
6,	Goa	2
7.	Gujarat	34
8.	Haryana	47
9.	Himachal Pradesh	15
10.	Jammu & Kashmir	19
11.	Karnataka	60
12.	Kerala	27
13.	Madhya Pradesh	44
14.	Maharashtra	65
15.	Manipur	1
16.	Meghalaya	2
17.	Nagaland	4
18.	Orissa	19
19.	Pondicherry	3
20.	Punjab	48
21.	Rajasthan	10
22.	Sikkim	3
23.	Tamil Nadu	60
24.	Tripura	2
25.	Uttar Pradesh	127
26.	West Bengal	49
	Total	820

14

Future Developments

Freedom from hunger was Gandhiji's priority number one for Independent India. To attain this objective, what we need now is an environmentally sustainable and socially equitable green revolution in our agriculture as it provides livelihood to 70 per cent population of the country. Just prior to our Independence, undivided India witnessed one of the most serious famines of this century–the great Bengal famine. Gandhiji speaking in Noakhali in 1946 said, "to the hungry God is bread" and "it is the duty of Independent India to ensure that every individual is enabled to earn his or her daily bread". Gandhiji's emphasis was on "food for all with human dignity". He did not want a nation of beggars or the entitlement to food being considered a charity. Thus, he asked us to desist from adopting a patronage approach towards the poor and hungry. Our first Prime Minister, Jawaharlal Nehru, responded to this call and announced in 1948 "everything else can wait but not agriculture"

We are now in the 50th year of our Independence. According to official statistics, about 200 million children, women and men will go to bed undernourished tonight. We have however successfully avoided famines during the last 50 years through a multipronged strategy consisting of (a) increased food production, (b) building grain reserves, (c) operating an extensive public distribution system, (d) protective social security measures like food for work, nutritious noon meal and employment guarantee, and (e) land reform and asset creation measures. The continued persistence of endemic hunger is now largely the result of inadequate purchasing power arising from inadequate opportunities for skilled employment.

Famines were frequent towards the part of the 19th century, when the combined population of India, Bangladesh and Pakistan was only 290 million. Our population alone is now more than thrice this number. Hence, we have every reason to be grateful for the spectacular success of the Government of India's famine avoidance and containment strategy. The time is now ripe to take the final steps essential for the total elimination of hunger. Hunger elimination is easier to achieve than poverty eradication. The poor spend a large share of their daily income on food and hence the elimination of hunger is the first step towards the alleviation of poverty. The opportunity for a productive and healthy life for every individual depends very much on the success of our hunger elimination strategy.

Economic regenration attempted in successive Five Year Plans has made agriculture a pride of national economy. This sector, today, provides livelihood to about 65 per cent of labour force, contributes n arly 29 per cent of Gross Domistic Product and accounts for a sizeable share of total value of the country's exports. It supplies bulk of wage goods required by non-agricultural sector and raw material for a large section of industry. Per capita net availability of foodgrains went up to a level of 468.5 grams per day in 1992 as compared to that of 395 grsams in early fifties. In 1994, it has, however, been provisionally estimated lower at 463.8 grams per day. In terms of gross fertilizer consumption, India ranks fourth in the world after USA, the erstwhile USSRand China. The country has the largest area in the world under pulse crops while in the field of cotton, India is the first to evolve a cotton hybrid.

Compound growth rate in agricultural production during the period 1949-50 to 1993-94 is 2.63 per cent per annum. Production of foodgrains increased significantly from 549.2 lakh tonnes in 1949-50 to 1,821 lakh tonnes in 1993-94. Cropping pattern is more diversified and cultivation of commercial crops has received new impetus in line with domestic demands and export requirements. During post-green revolution period i.e., 1967-68 to 1992-93, growth rate in agricultural production was assessed at around 2.84 per cent per annum. Production of foodgrains during this period increased from 950.5 lakh tonnes to 1,795 lakh tonnes. Cropping pattern has undergone perceptible changes and non-traditional crops like summer moong, soyabean, summer groundnut, sunflower, etc., are gradually gaining importance. In order to utilise scarce resources optimally, a short duration varieties have been introduced to use the residual moisture available from post-kharif and post-rabi cultivation.

The index of agricultural production, base TE 1981-82=100, which registered an increase of 21.4 per cent in 1988-89 and 2.1 per cent in 1989-90 over the previous year showed further increase of 3.8 per cent in 1990-91 due to increase recorded in the production of rice, wheat, pulses, oilseeds, jute and mesta, sugarcane and other commercial crops. During 1991-92, it, however, recorded a fall of two per cent due to fall in the production of various foodgrains but again registered an increase of 4.1 per centg due to increase in production of wheat coarse, cereals, pulses, ground-nut, cotton etc., during 1992-93 and again registered an increase of 2.8 per cent during 1993-94. The index of foodgrains production during 1993-94 at 148.9 showed an increase of 2.6 per cent over the previous year's production index of 145.1 Foodgrains production during 1992-93 increased by about 116 lakh tonnes over previous year's production primarily due to favourable weather conditions during the growth period of the crop. Availability of edible oils including vanaspati ha also increased significantly and its production in 1987 was 9,47,153 mt. The country has been able to sustain and improve availability of basic consumption articles and has thus, raised the standard of living.

There are three main crop seasons, namely, kharif, rabi and summer. Major kharif crops are rice, jowar, bajra, maize, cotton, sugarcane, sesame, soyabean and groundnut. Major rabi crops are wheat, jowar, barley, gram, linseed, rapeseed and mustard. Rice, maize and groundnut are grown in summer season also.

Land utilisation statistics are available for 92.8 per cent of total geographical area of 3,287.3 lakh hectare. According to land use statistics available from states, area under forests had increased from 404.8 lakh hectare in 1950-51 to 680.2 lakh hectare in 1992-92. Net sown area increased from 1,187.5 lakh to 1,414.1 lakh hectare during the same period. Broad cropping pattern indicates that though foodgrains, their relative share came down from 76.7 per cent during 1950-51 to 67.2 per cent during 1991-92.

Overall economic growth in terms of Gross Domestic Product (GDP) at constant factor cost improved from 0.8% in 1991-92 to 6.3% in 1994-95 and 7% in 1995-96 aided by a growth rate of 2.4% by agriculture and allied sectors, 11.7% by industry and construction sector and 7% by services. Overall economic growth during the first four year of the 8th Plan (1992-97) averaged 5.9% per annum compared with the planned target of 5.6%.

The domestic savings rate measured in terms of gross domestic savings as a proportion of GDP at current market prices increased from an average rate of 21.3% in 1992-93 and 1993-94 to 24.4% in 1994-95. The rate of domestic investment measured in terms of gross domestic capital formation as a proportion of GDP at current market prices increased from 21.6% in 1993-94 to 25.2% in 1994-95.

Industrial production which was virtually stagnant in 1991-92 increased by 9.4% and 12.1% in 1995-96 supported by a growth rate of 6.9% in mining, 13.6% in manufacturing and 8.1% in electricity generation. As per the latest information available, industrial growth deceleration to 8.5% in April-June 1996 due to deceleration of growth rates in all the sub-sectors (3.6% in mining, 10.4% manufacturing and 2.2% in electricity generation). As per growth rates by use-based classification, capital goods sector recorded a growth rate of 14.2%, intermediate goods 11.9%, consumer durables 11.1% and consumer non-durables 8.6% in April-June 1996. However, the growth rate of basic goods sub-sector having a weight of 39.4% in the overall industrial production was only 4% in April-June 1996.

Seven infrastructural sectors, namely, electricity, coal, steel, cement, crude oil and petroleum product & fertilizer with a combined weight of 31% in the Index of Industrial Production (IIP) recorded a growth rate of 7.8% in 1995-96. But their growth rate decelerated to 3.2% in April-August 1996 due to poor performance of electricity generation (growth rate of only 2.4%) and crude oil production (decline of production by 10.4%).

The outlook of agricultural production in 1996-97 is excellent with foodgrains output likely to reach 197 million tonnes compared with 185 million tonnes in 1995-96. This is primarily due to this year's rainfall distribution being the best in the past five years. The late withdrawal of monsoon has further ensured bright prospects for rabi production this year. The estimate of foodgrains production in 1995-96 has been scaled down to 185 million tonnes representing a sharp decline of nearly 6 million tonnes over the preceeding year. The shortfall was substantial (about 3 million tonnes) in wheat output, besides short-fall of production of rice and coarse cereals. Consequently wheat procurement dropped steeply to 8.2 million tonnes compared to 12.3 million tonnes in the preceding year. Public stock (Central Pool) of foodgrains was about 22.1 million tonnes as on September 1, 1996.

Challenge of hunger

The life and vitality of human beings depend crucially on certain vitamins and minerals that help in the efficient functioning of the brain, immune system, reproduction and energy metabolism. The body needs only small amounts of these nutrients, but it cannot synthesize them. They must be provided through diet. Deficiencies of even the small amounts required cause learning disabilities, impair work capacity and bring illness and death. Micronutrient malnutrition (silent hunger) is most devastating for pre—school children and pregnant women but is also debilitating for all ages. And it is debilitating the national economy as well. The most important and well studied micro-nutrient deficiencies are vitamin A, Iodine and Iron. Virtually every developing country has deficiencies in the micro nutrients large enough to constitute a public health problem. Many developing countries have multiple deficiencies. Taken together micronutrient deficiencies affect a far greater number of people in the world than Protein-Energy malnutrition. 1.6 billion people live in areas where soils lack sufficient iodine, 655 million suffer from goitre, 26 million have had brain damage and 5.7 million cretinism. Two billion pre-school children suffer from iron deficinet anaemia. 254 million pre-school children are affected by subclinical, severe and moderate deficiencies of Vitamin A.

In India, 167 millions are exposed to the risk of Iodine deficiency of which 54 million have goitre. Surveys conducted by DGHS indicate that 186 districts are IDD endemic area with goitre rates over 10 per cent. As regards Iron deficiency anaemia, multicentre study conducted by ICMR reveal that 87.5 per cent were anaemic. Deficiency of Vitamin A has long been known to be the largest preventable cause of blindness.

The main intervention strategies against micronutrient malnutrition are:

— Diet supplementation of vulnerable population.

— Dietary improvements.

— Fortification of common foods.

The richest sources of micronutrients are green leafy vegetable and fruits. India is rich in vegetable crops, some of which have good carotene content. Future programmes with respect to horticultural products must be directed towards identifying and propagating high micro-nutrient concentration varieties. People know when they are hungry but they have no natural hunger for vitamin. A, Iron, Iodine and other micronutrients. They do not know they need them and they often do not know what foods provide them.

Deficiency in soil nutrients reflect in the plants grown in the soil. One—half of all soils in all developing countries are deficient or low in available micronutrients. Soil depletion of S, Fe, Mn, Zn and Cu are due to intensive and indiscriminate irrigation and heavy use of high analysis chemical fertilisers. This gets reflected in the plants grown in these soils. Hence, in the national soil health care programme, we should ensure that both the macro-and micro-nutrient needs of soils are addressed.

The grim crisis, including a farmers' strike, over wheat procurement in Punjab and Haryana despite a hefty 25 per cent increase in purchase prices in a single year highlights the deep trouble brewing in our food economy. Already, the wheat buffer stock has plummeted to an alarming 2.7 million tonnes (mt), well below the recommended minimum of 3.7 mt, down from 12.9 mt just two years ago. Everything that the government has dome in the 1990s—from exporting grain when world prices are low, and importing when high, to raising procurement and issue prices unconscionably—speaks of gross mismanagement. If this continues, we could soon have Pakistan-style food riots. Already, the spectre of starvation and severe undernourishment stalks parts of Orissa, Maharashtra, Madhya Pradesh and Rajasthan. Our creaking public distribution system and its "targeted" variant, is in danger of collapsing. And yet there is irresponsible talk in policy circles of "unshackling" non-basmati rice exports and aligning domestic input and output prices with international levels.

That our food security should have been so badly undermined despite nine consecutive good monsoons speaks of a deep policy malaise and official callousness. The nineties have seen, for the first time in nearly four decades, foodgrain output growth lagging behind populaltion growth. Output growth has decelerated to less than half the 3.5 per cent rate of the 1980s. The slowdown is particularly severe in the case of rice and wheat, where the states that hold the key to marketable surpluses—and account for 80 per cent-plus of procurement—have witnessed a fall in growth rates to just 0.9 and 1.6 per cent, i.e. well below the population growth rate of 1.9 per cent. In our largest grain-producing state, paddy and wheat yields have fallen by 12 and 10 per cent respectively since 1992. Meanwhile, the output of "coarse" Meanwhile, the output of "coarse" cereals and pulses continues to shrink, eroding the food base of the poor, even as real farm wages decline.

Evidently, 30 years after it was launched, the Green Revolution has run its course or exhausted its potential, especially in the agriculturally most advanced areas. Northwestern India and parts of Andhra and Tamil Nadu show a clear trend of yields and output falling despite significant additions of inputs such as chemical fertiliser. Although eastern India has done relatively better, it simply can not compensate for the decline in the granary-states. In India as a whole, there are steeply falling returns to investment and inputs. As land is increasingly diverted to non-foodgrain uses, grain availability is further threatened. Given declining public investment in agriculture,—all this spells serious food insecurity.

Why has this happened? There are several reasons. First and foremost, the Green Revolution has come up against ecological and natural resources barriers. Its classic "package of practices" —high-yield (really high-response) seeds, big doses of irrigation, fertilisers and pesticides—backed by loans and guaranteed prices, is simply not sustainable in a natural-resources-poor society. In Punjab, 85 per cent of land has no more groundwater left to exploit. In Haryana, water-logging and salinity affect nearly a third of all land. In UP and Andhra, an overdose of chemicals is playing havoc with soil fertility. Farmers, who have oversaturated and killed lands with toxic chemicals, are now turning to nitrogen-fixing *dhancha* plants.

Secondly, unbalanced fertiliser use—encouraged by the Rs. 9,300 crore subsidy for urea—is playing havoc with soil health. The nitrogen-phosphorus-potassium ratio has changed to 8.5:6.6:1 in place of the optimal 4:2:1. (In UP, it is a dangerous 30:6:1). There is a severe and growing scarcity of micronutrients like zinc, copper, iron and manganese. A National Academy of Agricultural Sciences report warms of grave danger if micronutrients are not replenished and green-manuring not practised. Fertiliser overuse has been economically counterproductive too. Thus, fertiliser consumption has increased eight times over the past 25 years, but foodgrains output has not even doubled.

Third, the Green revolution's genetic breakthrough was largely limited to wheat and rice, which official policy favoured, while ignoring "coarse" grains)in reality, highly nutritious millets consumed by the poor). The result has been growing monocultures of rice and wheat, and loss of biodiversity. This also means inappropriate land-use: Punjab and Haryana, whose climate is unconducive to rice, have become its major producers. The Gangetic plains have turned into an environmentally unsustainable rice-wheat cropping system. Another consequence is sub-optimal use of water, and overuse of power, neither of which we can afford: the capital cost of major irrigation today is of the order of Rs. 50-80,000 per hectare. Servicing this annually alone would wipe out all profit from agriculture if the farmer were to bear the cost. He doesn't. The state does.

Fourth, in the nineties, the government deliberately changed its earlier policy of trying to keep food prices low. Following the premise that high output prices, and subsidised inputs would attract more investment and make agriculture competitive, it more than doubled the fertiliser subsidy. The idea was to "globalise" domestic prices for a specific crop spurt investment into its cultivation, but the aggregate supply response to an across-the-board increase in output prices is very weak.

Hence prices have risen, but investment, yield and output have not.

These processes/factors have resulted in a first-rate agrarian crisis. This crisis cannot be resolved by adding inputs, or promoting better fertiliser/pesticide use—i.e. more of the same. Dying land which has less then two per cent organic matter left in it cannot be revived by chemical means. There is no way that our electrical system can support the current 10-12 per cent annual increase in power consumption which water-intensive agriculture demands.

A paradigm shift is on order. we need a "Doubly Green revolution", which judiciously uses advances in plant genetics and biotechnology, but is simultaneously resource conserving and environmentally sound. This means a transition from high-energy, chemical-and water-intensive agriculture to low-input, low-chemical, more organic, waterconserving farming. It means altering the direction of breeding towards sturdy, drought-and-pest-resistant seeds based on indigenous genetic material and away from rice and wheat to millets, pulses and grasses. It means moving away from monocultures to plural agri-silvi-pastoral systems which recycle biomass. It means conserving energy. It means moving from big to small farmers.

Fortunately, we have a highly evolved agricultural research-and-extension system with the resources to undertake this transition. We must strengthen it, and discourage capital-and energy-intensive seed-breeding based on exogenous material. We must abandon the chimerical goal of "globalisation" and look at our own needs, endowments and knowledge systems. Such a paradigm shift alone can resolve today agrarian crisis.

New Delhi: If you live in the cities of India what you mostly hear about is what you haven't got but should be trying to: a better job perhaps your own flat, a new vehicle, or may be a credit card or a cell phone. Only now and again your eye may fall on newspaper stories about the wheat shortage or, if you are listening hard enough loud the rising prices and terrible shortage of atta in the market. You don't have to be a professional economist to tell that something must be very wrong if there is a foodgrain shortage after being repeatedly told that the country actually exports wheat, and also after hearing the Prime Minister's back-thumping sermon about India's self-sufficiency at the World Food Summit in Rome last month.

A couple of shocking statistics, recently released by the National Council of Applied Economic Research (NCAER) provide a horrific, if more accurate picture of where we are. The first figure is that 39 per cent of India's population of nearly one billion remains under the poverty line, a number that hasn't changed in a decade. In real terms this means that a very large number of Indians have an earning capacity of Rs. 5 or less a day, and are lucky to scratch up a meal of a couple of *chappatis*. According to another survey by the NCAER, 37 per cent of the country's rural population is landless and therefore unable to grow their own crop to fend off hunger.

The second figure, less published but available from international agencies, is that foodgrain production has been declining despite good monsoons—overall from 191 million tonne in 1994-95 to 185 million tonne in 1995-96 and in the case of wheat, from 65.5 million tonne to 62.6 million tonne in the same period. Unsurprisingly, the worst production shortfalls are in the politically volatile states of Uttar Pradesh and Bihar. Yet the naked face of hunger continues to be masked by the hypocrisy that India is an foodgrain exporter.

Still, there are plenty of Indians who want to know not merely how the government is in a position to export several million tonnes of wheat when there isn't enough to feed to the hungry, and then, to start importing two million tonnes to fill the ration shops when a widespread scarcity arises and prices begin to shoot up. A leader in The Economic Times last week argues that the government, the largest hoarder of foodgrains in the country, "is releasing large quantities in the country but not large enough quantities". It makes a strong claim for wheat imports to be put under Open General Licence amidst widespread speculation that the wheat shortage may be a repeat of last year's sugar scam and that the politicians could be back in the import-export business.

Even, if that is not the case, the situation is morally as indefensible as the problem of Indian children in labour—anywhere between 30 to 90 million depending on how you define "labour"—that the Supreme Court recently sought to curtail through stringent penalties. Surely the main reason why millions of our children are in bondage is to escape hunger?

Apart from the rising population, agro-economists put forward a number of reasons for falling production in foodgrains, among them soil exhaustion and the large number of landless that are concentrated in the states of UP, Bihar and eastern India. What they do not spell out is the endemic political instability and corruption in these states, and the interminable cycle of fodder scams and casts wars, that are pushing the poor deeper into the poverty trap. Economic reports do not point out that the agriculture ministry for many years has been managed by ministers like Devi Lal and Balram Jakhar, who only represent the narrow interests of wealthy landed farmers like themselves, and have no truck with the poor landless peasant. Devi Lal is chiefly remembered today for turning his ministerial bungalow and the Ashoka Hotel into a farmer's retreat while Balram Jakhar is the only ember of the PV Narsimha Rao's government involved inboth the *hawala* and *gawala* scams. It cost men like Jakahar nothing to proclaim that India should export pulses apart from wheat, knowing full well that production of pulses was dropping faster than that of wheat. The Deve Gowda government is heir to the same hypocrisy. The Prime Minister wants to impress the world about India's prestige as a wheat exporter but can do nothing about the gnawing pangs of hunger at home. Persisting shortages of food and soaring pricelines are not the result of natural causes alone. They are crises created by the men at the top.

Thirty years ago the Kalahandi region of Orissa had suffered a severe drought causing nearly a thousand deaths due to starvation and related diseases. The number of reported cases of starvation deaths in the current drought in the same area of Western Orissa may not exceed a dozen so far, but the magnitude of the crisis remains almost the same. Vulnerability of the people of this rainshadow area to crop loss and its consequences has hardly changed. Despite the visits of every Prime Minister of India, from Mrs Indira Gandhi to Mr H.D. Deve Gowda, to sypathise with the people and announce new projects, the basic conditions of poverty and underdevelopment have not changed.

Every 10 years there has been a severe drought and every third or fifth year has been a hard-hitting year of agricultural failure. Distress migration in mass scale, sale of household possessions and cattle and, condition of near starvation have been recurring in this region. In fact, as many as 26 out of Orissa's 30 districts have experienced over 50 per cent have experienced over 50 per cent crop loss this year and have been declared drought affected. The Kalahandi experience is a clear indictment of India's development path whether before or after liberalisation.

Failure of rains in the critical post-sowing months of June and July led to crop failure in this region. During My-October 1996 the recorded rainfall was only 632 mm against the average of 1217 mm. It is the erratic nature of the rainfall rather than its absence which upsets the farming process most of the time. The sprouts of paddy as usual dried up in June-July last year. While the traditional sources of water supply have disappeared new irrigation facilities have not sprung up. The worst affected districts of Bolangir and Nuapada (until recently a part of Kalahandi) are strewn with rivers and rivulets which overflow during the rainy season. They carry water into Mahanadi whose basin suffers from floods in the coastral area of Orissa practically every year.

Earlier people had their community tanks, bunds and small barrages to block river water. Slowly the affluent families and government established their control over these lands and used them for other purposes. Over the years community tanks went dry due to lack of public care. Currently only a small portion of cultivable land is irrigated by a few small reservoirs and lift irrigation projects.

During the past two decades the drinking water supply has considerably improved with the installation of tube wells. Even then visitors would see streams of women going to rivers to collect pots of water strained through sand as river water in this region tastes sweeter than underground water. People of the area have been demanding a number of small reservoirs from rivers and streams which would save rain water and tanks in specific spots in the area. this should be supplemented by deep borewells in some places. Lifting water from rivers and tanks through pumps should also be systematically arranged. In fact, an organisation called Sahavagi Vikas Abhijan has made a panchayat-wise study of the irrigation proposals made by the people.

In six blocks of Kalahandi-Nuapara region, which are chronically droughtprone, it has suggested 795 such projects, which would cost approximately Rs. 1,540 crore with a command area of nearly 1,15,000 hectares.

Very little has been done to chalk out a long-term strategy demanded by the people. The much trotted KBK (Longterm Action Plan for Kalahandi Bolangir Koraput region), formulated on the initiative of the PMO in 1993, put all the existing schemes and their allocations together for a five-year period amounting to nearly Rs. 5,000 crore. It is a point of ridicule in the eyes of the public and also the administration since it neither provides additional resources nor addresses the basic causes of the recurring crisis.

There has been some awakening—however marginal it may be among the people. In recent weeks there have been block office gheraos and rasta roko campaigns by people in some places demanding long-term measures to prevent recurrence of drought. Hopefully, the newly elected panchayat leaders will join the stream of awareness growing among the people of the region to carry on a new struggle for the basic human right to a livelihood. Experience shows that when people assert their right to control and utilise their resources then state and capital wake up to negotiate with them.

The term Green Revolution was coined by Dr. William Gadd of USA in 1968, when our farmers brought about a quantum jump in wheat production by taking to semi-dwarf, non-lodging varieties with great enthusiasm and when similar progress appeared feasible in rice. Punjab took the lead because of the scientific and educational backstopping given by the Punjab Agricultural University on the one hand and on the other, by the presence of the essential pre-requisites for progress such as land consolidation and leveling, rural communication, rural electrification and above all, owner cultivation.

Twenty eight years after the term "Green Revolution" was coined, we are in a position to draw a balance sheet and chalk out a strategy for the future. Apart from erasing the "begging bowl" image of India, the most important gain has been the saving of forests and land, thanks to the productivity improvement associated with high yielding varieties. This year, Indian farmers harvested over 60 million tonnes of wheat, as compared to 6 million tonnes at the time of our Independence in 1947. Punjab farmers have raised the average yield of wheat to over 40 quintals per hectare. Likewise, Tamil Nadu farmers have raised the average yield of rice to over 50 quintals per hectare. If the yield improvement associated with the Green Revolution in wheat and rice had not taken place, we will need another 70 million hectares to produce the wheat and rice we now harvest. Thus, the productivity inmprovement associated with the Green Revolution is best described as forest and land saving agriculture. The productivity improvement has taken place not only in wheat and rice but also in relation to milk and eggs. Only in the case of pulses, we are lagging behind.

The population of India is growing at a rate of 1.8 per cent per year. If this trend continues, our population will double itself in less than 40 years. Only Kerala, Tamil Nadu, Goa and Mizoram have so far achieved a demographic transition to low birth and death rates. Besides population increase, improved purchasing power among the poor will enhance the demand for food, since undernutrition and poverty go together. In contrast, per capita availability of arable land is shrinking. Water efficiency is still on the whole low and water disputes are growing. In addition to the gradual decline in per capita availability of land and water, various forms of biotic and abiotic stresses are spreading. There is still a widespread mismatch between production and post-harvest technologies. In perishable commotities like fruits, vegetables, flowers, meat and other animal products, this mismatch is often severe, affecting the inyterests of both producers and consumers. This is why foreign experts frequently refer to the setting in of a fatigue of the Green Revolution. Lester Brown and Hal Kane in their book "Full House" released last year p edict that at the current rate of population growth and environmental degradation coupled with an improvement in the consumption capacity of the poor, India will have to import annually over 40 million tonnes of food grains by the year 2030. This is four times the quantity we imported in 1966 i.e. before the onset of the Green Revolution. We should examine this issue seriously and should not allow complacency overtake the farm sector, just because we now have over 30 million tonnes of food grains available with Government.

Industrial countries are responsible for much of the global environmental problems such as potential changes in temperature, precipitation, sea level and incidence of ultraviolet-B radiation. While further agricultural intensification in industrialised countries will be ecologically disastrous, the failure to achieve agricultural intensification and diversification in developing countries where farming provides most of the jobs will be socially disastrous. This is because, agriculture including crop and animal husbandary, forestry and agro-forestry, fisheries and agro-industries provides livelihood to over 70 per cent of our population. The smaller the farm, the greater is the need for higher marketable surplus for increasing income. Eleven million new livelihoods will have to be created every year in India and these have to come largely from the farm and rural industries sectors. Importing food and other agricultural commodities will hence have the same impact as importing unemployment. Thus, what we need now is an environmentally sustainable and socially equitable green revolution or what may be termed as ever-green revolution.

Those who advocate going back to the old methods of farming ignore the fact that just a century ago when the population of undivided India was 281 million, famines claimed 30 million lives between 1870 and 1900. The famine eradication strategy of India comprising the following steps is perhaps the most important achievement of independent India:

— Enhanced production and productivity.

— Better distribution through the public distribution system.

— Adequate grain reserves.

— Purchasing power enhancement through various employment generation and guarantee schemes.

— Special intervention programmes for children, pregnant and nursing mothers and old and infirm persons.

While famines have been prevented, widespread under-nutrition prevails among the economically underprivileged. Since non-food factors like health care, environmental hygiene and literacy play an important role in promoting sustainable food security of the level of the individual we should redefine security.

Steps for achieveing sustainable food security are as under:

First sustained physical access to food will involve a transition from chemical and machnery intensive to ecological farming technologies.

Second, the emphasis on economic access underlines the need for promoting sustainable livelihoods through multiple income-earning opportunities.

Third, environmental access involves on the one hand attention to soil health care, water harvesting management and the conservation of forest and biodiversity, and on the other to sanitation, environment hygiene, primary health care and primary education.

If the political vision to implement this mission is forthcoming, population stabilisation can be more readily achieved. The prediction of Margins de Condorcet made in 1975 that population will stabilise itself, if children are born for happiness and not just for existence, will then come true.

The emphasis on the individual is important, since the household is not often a homogenous unit. Women and girl children tend to suffer more from under-nutrition than men and boys. UNDP's 1995 Human Development Report contains distressing data on the growing feminisation of poverty. To give operational content to such a concept of food security, we should initiate a Hunger-Free Area Programme (HFAP) consisting of the following components:

— Ensuring sustainable availability of food production over population growth through the development and dissemination of ecotechnologies, supported by appropriate packages of services and public policies. Ecotechnology involves the blending of the ecological prudence and technologies of the past, with the best in frontier technologies, particularly biotechnology, information technology, space technology, renewablre energy technology and management technology. Without ecotechnological empowerment, farm men and women will not be able to produce more food and other agricultural commodities on an environmentally sustainable basis from less land, water and energy resources.

— Sustain the productivity of the natural resource base, by conserving and improving the ecological foundations essential for continuous advances in crop and animal productivity.

— Ensure adequacy of household incomes through promotional social security, such as accessing assets, employment and organisational and marketing empowerment. Agricultural programmes should concurrently aim at more food, more jobs and more income. Integrated attention to farm and non-farm employment and value-addition to primary agricultural commodities will be necessary to enhance income and rural livelihood security.

— Provide entitlement to food through protective social security measures to the vulnerable groups, such as employment guarantee and food for nutrition programmes.

— Introduce a National Food and Livelihood Security Act for the purpose of paying integrated attention to:

Conservation of lands, water, forests, biodiversity and the protection of the atmosphere.

Enchancing productivity through ecotechnologies.

Improving distribution in order to eliminate endemic hunger.

Maintenance of adequate food security reserves.

Strengthneing the techno-infrastructure for better

post-harvest technology and expanding the coverage of sanitary and phytosanitary measures, and

Efficient research, education, extension, marketing systems both to take full advantage of emerging opportunities in international trade and to ensure that research and extension designed to promote public good receive adequate support.

Agricultural Growth

The rate of agricultural growth of the order of around 3.2 per cent per annum during the fifties was derived from acreage increases to the extent of 70 per cent. In the sixties, the rate of growth which was only 2.1 per cent in this sector and did not neutralize even the rate of increase of population in that decade, could be derived from acreage increase to the extent of 30 per cent only. The scope for any further increase in acreage for increasing agricultural peoduction has exhausted in the seventies and the entire increase in farm production had to come from improvement in per acre productivity. This has required high level of capital–intensive effort in the development of the agricultural sector.

According to a competent study, the capital output ratio in Indian agriculture has already touched the figure of four and is close to the same scale as is required in industry. For the same reason, the fact has to be reckoned with that absorption of labour in agriculture through a significant rise in yields on land has tended to be a comparatively limited and expensive process and this process alone cannot be relied upon to solve the growing unemployment problem. The running controversy on priorities as between agriculture and industry, in particular heavy industry, is thus futile and misleading in the context of the realities of Indian economic situation and its growth prospects. The idea that India enjoys a comparative advantage in agricultural output inIndia is now crucially dependent on growth of inputs from industry.

The need is thus not to fforeclose available resources in the economy for the so called development needs of the agricultural sector but to mop up a substained part of the surpluses and incremental incomes generating in the agricultural sector to meet the investment requirements of infrastructural development, including heavy and intermediate goods industries,to inputs for agriculture at a rapid and accelerating pace.

If much credit is taken for achieving self—sufficiency in food grains relative to effective domestic demand, there is now much brave talk of making India one of the few "grain powers" in the world even while large number of Indian people still do not have access to adequate food. Agriculture in India will have to go a long way yet before it can feed the Indian people. It is too early to talk of India becoming a "grain power." But the official policy has already veered to the postion that the government would not come in the way of the farmers exporting their produce and these exports would not be banned "merely" for bringing supplies and prices down for the domestic consumers. The upshot has been that while good grains have been exported, two million tonnes of wheat are being imported in the current year, 1996—97 to meet even the effective demand in the domestic market. The danger inherent in this position is not imaginary.

The widening disparities in incomes and levels of living combined with growing concentration of land and the swelling ranks of landless rural labourers are manifest. It is not amiss either to consider the pricing of agricultural produce, more especially food grains—the primary wage goods—and examine its influence on the general price trend and structure of relative prices in the Indian economy. The Agricultural Prices Commission, to start with, recommended a particular set of prices based on its studies of the cost of production, fair return to the farmer and fair prices for the consumer.

It has been a practice, by and large, to improve upon the prices recommended by the APC in order to provide additional incentives to the surplus farmers to increase production for the market. After the launching of the so—called economic reforms in 1991, however, the baalance between the claims of the surplus farmer and the consumer has been tilting sharply in favour of the former and the inflationary impact of "incentive prices" for good grains and other agricultural produce has been ignored. Subsidised farming by way of what are called "incentive prices" for farm produce and subsidised inputs for agriculture like chemical fertilizers, private irrigation facilities like tubewells and pumpsets, power andcomparative soft—term credit, was conceived in the wake of the disastrous drought years of 1964-65 as the means of stimulating agricultural production for the market and securing control over a substantial part of the marketable surpluses so produced.

There were probably compelling reasons under the given ownership pattern in cultivable land for adopting this strategy when shortages of agricultural commodities, especially of food grains, ad emerged as an endemic problem of the economy—its stability and further growth. But the concomitant of this development has been the growing commercialization of agriculture and emergence within it to prominence of that segment of farmers with their commercial interests which produce and control agricultural surpluses. In the course of time, however, as shortage in cereals or other crops are overcome relative, of course, to effective market demand at the present low-level of purchasing power in the economy, the system of subsidised production and marketing in agriculture has become in essence a mechanism to ensure to the surplus producer a monopoly to all the gains arising from incrreases in production and productivity.

Among the vast numbers of Indian farmers, only a small fraction, and more than 10 per cent of the total, commanding the best cultivable land produces for the market on any scale. They also monopolise the subsidised supply of inputs and credit and benefits of infrastructural facilities such as irrigation and power created by public investment.

The official planners have been very brave, indeed foolhardy, to scale up from 3.5 per cent to 4.5 per cent, reportedly under political pressure, the agricultural growth rate target for the Ninth Plan. This may please the powerful lobby of rich farmers and pander to their high growth ambitions. But it casts grave doubts on the veracity and credibility of the planning exercise, especially so when the sharp set-back to agricultural production in 1995-96, a good monsoon year, should have made the planners doubly cautious in their approach to the ticklish problems and uncertain prospects of Indian agriculture.

Disturbing trends

The disturbing indications that really must hot be ignored cavalierly are that the Green Revolution in irrigated areas based on viable farmers and subsidized inputs especially chemical fertilizers, may have touched the plateau. Also to reckon with is the shrinking social base of farming, with small and marginal farmers being squeezed out and the big gentlemen farmers with large land holdings and access to modern inputs and technologies furiously developing a nexus with urban business corporations, including multinational corporations. The agricultural growth target of 4.5 per cent for the Ninth Five Year Plan may, in this context, make some sense only if it is projected not for the total production or food security for the people of India, especially half the population suffering from poverty, hunger and malnutrition, but for marketable surpluses to meet effective demand, that is demand backed by purchasing power for agricultural products, including food grains, in the domestic and the global markets.

The performance of Indian agriculture after gaining political independence has been impressive and should not be derided as has been done by the votaries of the market-oriented growth of industry as well as agriculture. Food production quadrupled between 1951 and 1991. There was also significant growth of what are known as case crops to augment supplies for a wide variety of processing industries. This success was achieved with positive intervention of the Indian State, including large public investment in irrigation, research and development and, supplies of subsidized inputs like quality seeds, fertilizers and power. This was combined with judicious support prices for agricultural produce, especially food grains. Since the launching of the so-called economic reform policies in 1991 to bring about what is loftily claimed to be the structural adjustment of the Indian economy, the position of Indian agriculture has changed ominously. The fluctuations in agriculture production have become sharper. There is shift away from food grains to cash crops. Within the food crops, production of rice and wheat has been given generous price and other incentives. The production of coarse cereals, pulses and grains has tended to decline. With the per capita availability of cereals declining, the poor have been hit hard by their rising prices. The nature and content of agricultural growth has not even been properly comprehended, let alone tackled in the approach paper on the Ninth Plan.

New strategy in the sixties

A marked feature of agricultural policy or what is known as the new agricultural strategy launched in the mid-sixties was a decisive shift of emphasis from institutional reform to technological improvement. This found expression in the organization of modern inputs for viable farming. Expansion of irrigation, especially on private account, and supply of chemical fertilizers, pesticide and quality seeds registerd a relatively big advance and helped to enhance production and productivity of farmers with addess to these facilities. Since the farmers with marketable surpluses were at the same time assured of rising levels of incentive-procurement prices, the govenment was able, side to mop up adequate qualities of agricultural produce, especially of food grains, for current consumption well as building up of the buffer stocks.

The problem of feeding the urban population and the growing non-agricultural force was acute in the fifties and the sixties. This was indeed the biggest stumbling block in the way of overall economic stability and growth. Reliance on aided imports of food grains necessarily imposed sever strains, economic and political. It may well be claimed that Indian agriculture has by now developed to a point where it is in a position to meet effective demand for food grains in the Indian market. In this sense, the agrarian crisis as it manifested itself till the mid-seventies can be said to have been resolved. But the question now to be faced is the further growth of agriculture, its content and direction.

It is not without significance either that land reforms are no longer projected in official policy as an essential prerequisite for overcoming bottlenecks to higher production and productivity in agriculture. They are at best treated as desirable purely from the social justice angle. The talk of land reforms which the political leaders indulge in from time to time is, is therefore more of a populist gesture that carries little conviction in the political power system.

The prospect of growth in agriculture in 1996-97 appears to be excellent and the year is likely to end up with foodgrains production of over 191.2 million tonnes as against 185 million tonnes in the preceding year. In commercial crops, particularly oilseeds, and cotton, significant increase in output is quite certain. The only area of concern, however, is the continued slow growth in production of pulses. Overall, the agriculture production is likely to record a growth rate of about 3 per cent in 1996-97.

1996 was the ninth successive normal monsoon year. Country wide seasonal rainfall was 103 per cent of the long—term average which was better than that of last year. The monsoon arrived almost on time and covered the entire country by June 30, two weeks earlier than the normal date. By the end of the Monsoon season (June-September),32 out of 35 meterological sub-division and 81 per cent of districts covering 91 per cent area of the country had received normal to excess rainfall. The comparative performance of the monsoon for the past ten years, 1987 to 1996. The district-wise distribution of rainfall for the past 10 years.

The spatial and temporal rainfall distribution over the country was very satisfactory except over Orrissa and Vidarbha where rainfall was marginally deficient or scanty in some districts. In the later part of June, Rajasthan and Haryana experienced floods. In third week of July, floods also occured in north Bengal and Bihar.

Excessive rain due to cyclonic storm caused extensive damage twice in Andhra Pradesh, first in June and then again in early November.

Total rainfall, its spatial and temporal distribution and its impact on the production of Kharif cereals, can be seen from the rice area and production weighted rainfall index constructed for each State and aggregated over All India. Cereals production weighted cumulative rainfall indices for the entire season are computed by assigning weights based on share in the production of kharif cereals. A comparative picture of temporal distribution of rainfall during the sout-west monsoon season of 1996 as compared to 1995 and 1994.

Rabi prospects also depend to some extent on post monsoon rainfall. The cumulative rainfall during the post sout-west monsoon season 1996 (1 October to 31 December) was excess or normal in 25 meteorological sub-divisions as against 16 subdivisions during the corresponding period last year. Performance of the post-monsoon rainfall for the past 6 years.

The main states or division which received deficient or scanty rainfall during the post monsoon period are Gangetic West Bengal, Sub-Himalayan West Bengal and Sikkim, Orissa, Bihar Plateau, Jammu & Kashmir, Himachal Pradesh, Punjab, Haryana, Chandigarh, Delhi, Hills of West Uttar Pradesh and East Madhya Pradesh.

The total live storage position in 63 important reservoirs in different part of the country by the end of September, 1996 as monitored by the Central Water Commission was much better this year. It was 97.7 Thousand Million Cubic Meters (TMC) at the end of September, 1996 as against 90.1 TMC during the corresponding period of 1995. Comperative position of storage level at the end of September, 1996.

Agriculture production performance in the last five years together with the prospects for 1996-97.

Foodgrains account for about 63 per cent of country's agricultural output and hence even a marginal decline in foodgrains production has a 'ripple effect' on rest of the economy. Despite a near normal monsoon in 1995, the foodgrains output of 185 million tonnes in 1995-96 was lower by over 6 million tonnes. This was mainly on account of decrease in production of wheat, kharif rice, bajra and pulses. The most unexpected development was the late realisation in 1996 that the wheat harvest was just about 62.6 million tonnes, lower by about 3 million tonnes over the preceding year. The reasons for decline in production of rabi foodgrain crops i.e. wheat conditions at the grain filling stage of the crop in February/March, 1996. This was a serious set back and its late realisation did cause some distortions in wheat availability. Wheat prices rose to unprecedented heights by November, 1996, promoting the Government to release larger quantities from FCI's public stocks besides taking recourse to imports. Kharif 1996 foodgrains output is likely to be 103.2 million tonnes as against only 98.2 million tonnes in 1995. If Rabi crops prospects turn out to be normal, 1996-97 foodgrains output is likely to be 191.2 million tonnes which would be close to the record production of 191.5 million tonnes achieved in 1994-95. The annual growth rate in foodgrain production in recent past.

Per hectare yield rates of rice and wheat rose significantly during seventies and eighties. Consequently, both these foodgrains registered over 3 over per cent annual growth in production between 1980-81 to 1995-96, which was significantly higher than the annual population growth of 2.14 per cent during eighties. The low annual growth of 1.2 per cent in production of pulses since 1980-81 did, however, looking at the first seven years of this decade (1990-91 to 1996-97), the annual rate of growth of foodgrains was only 1.7 per cent which is lower than the current population growth. If this trend continues it could become a matter of grave concern.

Rice production reached a record level of 81.8 million tonnes in 1995 However, production in 1995-96 was down to 79.6 million tonnes. Production in Kharif, 1996 is estimated to be 70.6 million tonnes compared to 70.1 million tonnes in Kharif, 1995. Some adverse impact on rabi/summer rice during 1996-97 on account of the deficient/scanty rains, particularly in Orissa and West Bengal and also on account of cyclonic strom in Andhra Pradesh, has been reported. Despite this, if 1996 Rabi rice output remains at 1994-95 or 1995 or 1995-96 level of around 9 million tonnes, the total output of rice may be 79.6 million tonnes in 1996-97.

Wheat output of 62.6 million tonnes in 1995-96 was 3.2 million tonnes lower over 1994-95 output of 65.8 million tonnes. Due to sudden rise in temperature at the grain filling stage of the crop in February/March, 1996, there was an unexpected decline in its productivity in major wheat growing States except Haryana and Rajasthan. Service incidence of yellow rust was also reported on wheat variety HD-2329 which is largely grown in Punjab. 1996-97 target of wheat output is 65 million tonnes. The weather parameter of temperature was initially low, which is considered beneficial for the crop growth. However, delayed winter rains in the wheat growing area have resulted in moisture stress conditions. If the rainfall/temperature conditions are normal in the Rabi season, the production of wheat may be relatively better and could be expected at around 64.50 million tonnes in 1996-97. Wheat is becoming important even in rice consuming areas and increasingly subsituting for coarse cereals as urbanisation and incomes rise. The ratio of wheat production to rice production has steadily increased from one third in 1950-51 and 1960-61 to about one half in 1970-71 and further to four fifth in 1995-96.

The area under coarse grains (bajra, maize, jowar, ragi, small millets and barley) continues to show a declining trend and stagnation in production. Coarse grains are mostly grown by small and marginal farmers in areas largely characterised by low and erratic rainfall. The coarse grains are grown mostly in Maharashtra, Rajasthan, Madhya Pradesh, Uttar Pradesh, Andhra Pradesh, Tamil Nadu and Bihar. In 1995-96, the production of all the coarse cereal crops except bajra was relatively better than 1994-95. The production of bajra in 1995-96 suffered badly in the major States of Rajashtan, Gujarat, Haryana and Maharashtra and was 5.39 million tonnes i.e. substantially lower by 24.7 per cent over the production level of 7.16 million tonnes achieved in 1994-95. Despite this, the production of coarse cereals is estimated to be 29.1 million tonnes in 1995-96. As the rainfall and weather situation, particularly during the monsoon period, has been quite favorable in the major coarse cereal growing States, the production prospects have improved and the coarse cereal out is expected to be about 33.05 million tonnes in 1996-97.

Pulses production in the country has been stagnating around 8-14 million tonnes for the last 40 years. Per capital availability of pulses has come down from 69 grams in 1961 to about 39 grams in 1996. Production fluctuates from year to year depending on the performance of monsoon. The practice of inter cropping and mixed cropping is also more prevalent in pulses, which are grown as secondary crops. The production of pulses, which crossed 14 million tonnes in 1995-96. This was due to the substantial fall in production of gram to 5.02 million tonnes in 1995-96 from a level of 6.44 million tonnes in the preceding year. This shortfall was, however, offset to some extent by higher production achieved in Tur and other pulses in 1995-96. As a result of better monsoon rainfall, the production of pulses is expected to be higher and may be around 14 million tonnes in 1996-97.

The production of commercial crops like sugarcane (283 million tonnes), oilseeds (22.4 million tonnes) cotton (13.1 million bales) have been of a record level in 1995-96. As per the present assessment, the production prospects of these crops are better in 1996-97 and the production may go up further.

Sugarcan production reached a record level of 275.54 million tonnes in 1994-95 surpassing its earlier record level of 254 million tonnes of 1991-92. Again, a record production of 283 million tonnes of sugarcane has been estimated for 1995-96. Current production prospects of sugarcane are also quite good and is expected to be about 274 million tonnes in 1996-97.

Sugar production reached an all time record level of about 164 lakh tonnes in sugar year 1995-96 (October, 1995 to September, 1996), recording a substantial jump over the precedng years of record production of 146 lakh tonnes. Two years of record output of sugar has resulted in accumulation of sizable stocks, and industry is striving to export more, depending upon whether the global prices are favorable. The Statutory Minimum Price (SMP) for sugarcane for 1995-96 was fixed at Rs. 42.50 per quintal linked to a basic recovery of 8.5 per cent and for the 1996-97 season it has been fixed at Rs. 45.90 per quintal.

The sugar industry continues to function under a regulatory system where licences have to be sought for establishing new capacity or expanding the existing installed capacity. There is also a dual price control system under which 40 per cent of output is pre-empted for use of the government for PDS, at an ex-factory price which is fixed for each of 16 Zones. The balance 60 per cent output, factories are free to sell at the market price except that the quantity for free sale is regaulated by precscribing monthly quantities that each units can sell as non-levy sugar.

During the financial year 1995-96, the releases for PDS ranged from 3.27 to 4.03 lakh tonnes per month. Similarly, the releases for freesale sugar were kept high between 6.25 to 8.30 lakh MTs per month so as to ensure that freesale market price of sugar remained at a reasonable level. The stock holding limits and turnover period of sugar and khandasari were enhanced to 1000 quintals and 30 days from 1st October, 1996 from 500 quintals and 15 days respectively to promote increased availability of sugar in the market.

During the 1995-96 sugar season, about 8.87 lakh tonnes of sugar was exported. Sugar export has been decanalized and manufacturing units are now permitted to pack sugar in 50 kg. packages for export purposes and from 5th November, 1996, also in small consumer packs of 1, 2 and 5 kgs. for indigenous use. These packages can be made from any foodgrade packaging material.

Among the nine oilseed crop grown in the country, groundnut and rapeseed/mustard together for 62 per cent of total oilseeds production. Soyabean and sunflower have to late emerged as the oilseed crops having major growth potential. The other oilseed crops include seasamum, castorseed, nigerseed, safflower linseed. Oilseeds production was 18.61 million tonnes in 1990-91 and has since touched a level of 22.42 million tonnes in 1995-96. The production in 1996-97 is likely to be 24.11 million tonnes.

Cotton production is estimated at 130.9 lakh bales of

170 kgs. each in 1995-96, and increase of 10.1 per cent over the production of 118.9 lakh bales in 1994-95. Due to increase both in area coverage and its productivity, the production of cotton is likely to go up further in 1996-97 an is expected to be around 143 lakh bales.

Production of Jute and Mesta continued to stagnate. Production which had reached a record level during 1995-86, registered a sharp decline and hovered around 6.78 to 10.29 million bales thereafter. Production in 1995-96 is expected to be 8.90 million bales, and may rise marginally to 9.19 million bales in 1996-97.

Crop production

Agricultural crop production in 1996—97 is expected to show good recovery from the slower growth in 1995—96. Growth is projected at 3 per cent after a fall of 0.4 per cent in 1995—96. The sharp decline in foodgrains production by 3.4 per cent, which was responsible for the slow growth in 1995—96, is expected to be reversed by an increased of 3.3 per cent in 1996—97. Foodgrains production is expected to recovery is primarily due to coarse cereals, as well as an anticipated rise in wheat production which suffered a sharp setback in 1995—96.

As the agricultureal year runs from July to June, the estimates for 1995—96 were only firmed up after the end of the financial year. A large downward revision (of 3 million tonnes) was made in the estimate of wheat production for 1995—96. The revision was unexpected and unexplained, because average rainfall in 1995—96 was quite normal. The revision, late in calendar year 1996, also created severe problems for the management of the food economy.

Commercial crop production has done extremely well in 1996—97 with oilseeds and cotton expected to reach record levels of 24.1 million tonnes and 14.3 million tonnes, respectively. Jute and mesta have also shown a growth of 3.4 per cent this year. Sugarcane output is, however, unlikely to maintain the record level of 283 million tonnes attained in 1995—96.

Industrial production (as measured by the index of industrial production–IIP), grew by 9.8 per cent in the first seven months of 1996—97, 1.9 percentage points slower than the 11.7 per cent growth in the in the corresponding period of 1995—96. The good performance of industrial production in 1996—97 is due entirely to the manufacturing sector, which has maintained its high growth.

The slowing of industrial production is clearly attributable to the dramatic fall in the rate of growth of electricity production and a slowing of growth in the mining sector mainly because of the 10 per cent decline in crude oil production. During the first seven months of 1996—97, electricity production (as measured by the index) has grown by only 3.4 per cent compared to the 10.1 per cent growth in the corresponding period of 1995—96. It is somewhat surprising that manufacturing sector growth has been barely affected by the slow growth in electricity production. One possibility is that captive electricity generation, which is increasingly used as a back—up to public supply, has substituted for the lack of generation by electricity boards. The high growth of diesel imports, about 22 per cent by volume in the first seven months of 1996—97 (with total refinery throughput growing in the normal range of around 4 per cent), is consistent with this hypothesis. At present, electricity statistics incorporate little or no data on captive power generation.

Another noteworthy aspect of industrial growth this year is the acceleration in the rate of growth of capital goods production to 16.6 per cent in the first seven months of this year from 15 per cent in the first seven months of last year. This has off—set the decline in the rate of growth of consumer goods and basic goos. In contrast, capital goods imports have declined by 6 per cent in the first seven months of 1996—97. This shows the increased competitiveness of the domestic capital goods industry. The overall performance of the core and infrastructure sectors during the first 8 months of 1996—97 (April—November) has been poor.

Six industries namely, electricity generation, coal, steel, crude oil, petroleum products and cement, with a combined weight of 28.8 per cent in the Index of Industrial Production (IIP), averaged a growth of 4.1 per cent in April—November, 1996, less than half the 8.9 per cent, in April—November, 1995. The deceleration in the growth rate of these infrastructure industries is mainly due to a decline in crude oil production and power generation. Hydro power generation declined by 7.7 per cent, and thermal power generation grew by only 6.4 per cent in the April—November, 1996 as compared to 14.6 per cent in the April—March, 1995—96. Coal, cement and refineries' throughput have grown faster in April—November, 1996—97 compared to the corresponding period of 1995—96. Growth of sectors such as railways, ports and telecommunications, which do not appear in the IIP, also slowed. The rate of growth of railways' revenue earning goods traffic decelerated marginally from 7 per cent during 1995—96 to 6.3 per cent for April–November 1996. Growth of cargo handled at major ports and new telephone connections provided decelerated more sharply to 4.7 per cent in April—November, 1996 (from 9.1 per cent in 1995—96) and 8.3 per cent in April—November, 1996 (from 23.3 per cent in 1995–96), respectively. The slower growth in cargo handled by ports in probably the result of a deceleration in the growth of external trade. The telecomunications slowdown, however, suggests that the pace of implementation of telecommunications reform needs to be accelerated and its scope widened to include Department of Telecommunications as a service provider. Given the parlous financial state of many public utilities, particularly the State Electricity Boards, the possibility of crises worsens with each passing year. The new government has repeatedly stressed its firm determination to reform the infrastructure and energy sectors. In line with this commitment, a number of policy decisions have been taken and new initiatives launched.

The second International Crop Science Congress, held in New Delhi from November 17 to 24, has displayed the International scientific community's will to solve the mankind's basic problem of hunger and to lay the foundation for a vibrant, yet ecologically sustainable, agriculture to meet future needs. The world's largest assembly of crop scientists, over 1500 from nearly 70 countries, emphasised that the modern biotechnology, coupled with traditional wisdom, can mould future to suit the interest of the human society. Though new challenges will keep cropping up, the science would perhaps not only be able to deal with them but might indeed convert them into opportunities for the good of humanity.

The optimism would, however, hold true only if it is matched by political will to raise farm productivity as also to distribute its gains equitably. New technology accompanied by appropriate marketing policies and international cooperation holds the key to ensuring foods security in the years to come.

Deliberations of the mega scientific event, organised jointly by the National Academy of Agricultural Sciences (NAAS) and the Indian Council of Agricultural research (ICAR), once again confirmed the widely held notion that while the scientists would be able to cope with humanity's needs they may become helpless to cope with its greed. The world renowned agricultural expert, Dr. M.S. Swaminathan, who chaired the Congress, did not mince words in passing on this message. He said: "Whether in agriculture or aquaculture, we must curb the greed revolution and promote an ever-green revolution capable of bringing about continuous advances in terrestrial and aquatic productivity without harm to the environmental capital stocks of land, water forests, biological diversity, oceans and climate upon which such advances depend."

The theme of the Congress, "Crop productivity and sustainability—shaping the future"—was highly appropriate and topical for several reasons. Despite phenomenal growth in food production, nearly one-fifth of the world population is still malnourished and hungry. The impact of the green revolution is waning and concerns of productivity decline in major crop production systems are being expressed globally, diminishing per capita availability of land and water resources, expanding biotic and abiotic stresses and natural resources, including land, forest and environment, are fast degrading. This calls for greater resolve to ensure synergism among productivity, profitability and sustainability of major cropping systems. Moreover, for safeguarding food and nutritional security at the household level, crop intensification and diversification are needed on an ecologically sustainable basis.

Let us now concentrate on another important aspect, e.g. the impact of Operation Barja on production. During 1972—73 to 1978—80 the foodgrain production in West Bengal grew at a rate of 1.7% as against 2.5% for India as a whole. During the decade of eighties, i.e. the post operation Barga period, the growth of food grain production in West Bengal was 3% as against India's

2.4% (Sengupta 1993). During this period West Bengal has also seen an increase in oilseeds and potato production. Although a large part of this increase may be the field of agriculture, the role of land reform in boosting agriculture cannot be totally denied. There are studies which show that the productivity of share cropped land is higher for recorded than for unrecorded share croppers (Chandra 1993).

A micro level survey conducted by Chaudhuri and Pal (1993) reveals that the productivity of self cultivated owned land is higher than that of land under share cropping arrangement (both recorded and unrecorded). The study also reveals that the use of input e.g. chemical fertilizers and high yielding variety (HYV) of seeds ar also lower in tenant operated plots. One possible reason is the poverty of the tenants which makes them incapable of purchasing fertilizer and necessary irrigation water for cultivation of HYV crops. Moreover there may be reluctance on the part of the share—croppers to invest more on a leased in plot whose output will have to be shared with the owner.

So far as the distribution of vested land is concerned, West Bengal has performed very well. At the end of 1991, 0.37 million hectares of land were distributed among 2.0 million families. In West Bengal, the two schemes, i.e. the distribution of surplus land and recording of Barga cover nearly 40% of the rural households. Most of the holdings are rainfed and hence it is not possible to raise Rabi or Boro crops on the plot. The scarcity of irrigation water affects the recorded share croppers equally. Another important problem of the owners of vested land is the scarcity of bullock power to till land. These people have to hire bullock and carts from their landlords and this may, in some cases, lead to exploitation by landlords.

The problems discussed so far may be eased by establishing cooperatives for agricultural inputs specially irrigation and bullock power. One obstacle to the formation of such cooperatives is fragmentation of land. The consolidation of holdings has not been done in most of the states.

At present the owners of adjacent holding may form groups for investing in shallow tubewells, pumpsets, bullocks and carts. In order to utilize a pair of bullocks an average of 4 to 5 acres of land is required. So formation of cooperatives is the easiest way of utilising the bullock power most economically. Tractors may also b purchased and maintained on a cooperative basis. For the success of cooperative movement special attention should be given to the consollidation of fragmented holdings.

The owners of marginal plots and also the poor share croppers should be trained properly to start various off—farm activity, e.g. cottage industries, animal husbandary, pisciculture etc. These off—farm activities will be their secondary sources of income. Loans and subsidies should also be made available to this group for starting such off—farm activities. All these will go a long way to make the land reform measures a success.

Food consumption

Against the per capita net availability of 501.9 gms of cereals the estimated consumption of cereals was of the order of 394 gms i.e. 78.6 per cent of the net availability. similarly in the case of pulses, per capita consumption was 28.05 gms. i.e. 75.8 per cent of net availability. Inequality in the consumption of foods among different income groups gets masked in the overall consumption estimates. Among the poor, nearly 80 per cent of consumption expenditure goes for food items. Recent surveys indicate:

— Percapita cereal consumption has declined over the years resulting in the aggregate energy intake of 1859 k.cal per capita as against 2200 k.cal recommended.

— 47.7 per cent of households have calorie inadequacy and 19.8 per cent of households have protein inadequacy. 19.5 per cent of households have both calorie and protein inadequacy.

— The exetent of moderate and severe growth retardation in preschool children varied from 34 per cent in Kerala to 72 per cent in Gujarat.

— 47 per cent of adults have body mass index value below 18.5 indicating large scale prevalance of chronic energy deficiency in the community.

— Haemoglobin levels among pregnant mothers reveal that as many as 87.5 per cent of mothers were anaemic.

— About 30 per cent of infants born had low birth weight.

— 167 million people are considered to be at risk for iodine deficiency disorders and 54 million have goitre.

— Preventable blindness due to Vitamin A deficiency still large.

Looking back the distance travelled and counting on various milestones towards food security, the country can be proud of some of the achievements so far. Yet the final milestone looks to be a long march. Shrinking arable land resources, soil degradation and depletion of nutrients from the soil, poor water management and unsustainable use of ground water, loss of momentum in the growth of food output, inefficient biological utilisation of the nutrients consumed due to poor environment and growing population are some of the problems the country faces in the march towards the final milestone of a hunger-free nation. The over-exploitation of the aquifer is also leading to the leaching of high levels of arsenic from natural underground sources into thousands of village wells in West Bengal. As estimated 200,000 people already have arsenic-induced skin lesions. It is estimated that there are about 20 million species of poants, out of which 50,000 are edible. However, we are not using more than 200 plants as food, 80 per cent of our food supply however comes only from about eight species. We are today laying much emphgasis on developing new varieties of these few plants. We should enlarge the food basket by including the excluded. Many nutritious grains fall under the classification "coarse grains". It is time we start referring to them as "nutritious grains". They are rich in micronutrients like Fe and Ca.

The momentum of growth witnessed in 1995—96 with a GDP growth of over 7 per cent, has been maintained in 1996—97, thus providing increasing evidence that the growth potential has improved as a result of the reforms initiated in 1991. With the growing participation of virtually the entire spectrum of political opinion inthe reform process, there is a good prospect that a higher growth rate would become a permanent feature of the economy.

The initial spurt of reforms from 1991—92 to 1993—94 was very successful by all accounts, resulting in a jump in economic growth to 7.2 per cent in 1994—95 (in terms of GDP at factor cost). Since 1994—95, however, there was a marked slow down in the pace of reforms. Nevertheless, GDP grew by 7.1 per cent in 1995—96. The slackening of reforms preceding and during the election period may have been responsible for some loss of momentum, but this has been revived with a series of measures in recent months.

Economic growth in 1996—97 is estimated by CSO to be around 6.8 per cent (GDP at factor cost). Thus, the Eighth Plan is likely to end with an average growth of 6.5 per cent per annum, 0.9 per cent point higher than the target rate of 5.6 per cent, and 0.5 per cent point higher than the actual achievement of the Seventh Plan. More important for the future is the fact that the average growth during the latest three years is 7 per cent, probably placing India among the top ten performers in the world during this period.

As the final year of the Eighth Plan draws to a close, a comparison of some salient dimensions of some salilent dimensions of economic performance between the Eighth Plan period and its predecessor reveals the following:

— Overall economic growth has been faster;

— The manufacturing sector has grown almost 2 per cent points faster per year in the Eighth Plan period;

— Agriculture and allied sectors have grown at about 3.5 per cent per annum in both periods;

— Both exports and imports have grown significantly faster in the Eighth Plan period;

— The balance of payments has strengthened considerably, with trade and current account deficits declining as ratios of GDP, while exports and imports have grown rapidly both in value terms as well as in proportion to GDP.

— The Central Government's fiscal deficit as a proportion of GDP has declined significantly;

— The average rate of gross domestic savings has risen substantially from 20.6 per cent of GDP in the Seventh Plan period to 23.9 per cent in the first four years of the Eighth Plan;

— With the exception of telecommunications, the rate of growth of net output (value added) of infrastructure sectors has slowed;

— The average rate of inflation has risen somewhat, though remaining below double digits.

Total gross domestic saving reached a new peak of 25.6 per cent of GDP in 1995—96, exceeding its previous peak of 24.9 per cent of GDP in 1994–95. This seems to vindicate the reform strategy of encouraging savings by expanding saving and investment opportunities, rather than giving special incentives.

Gross domestic investment (adjusted), as a proportion of GDP at current prices, rose even faster than gross domestic saving in 1995—96 to a high of 27.4 per cent from 26 per cent in the previous year. Gross domestic investment in real terms, as a proportion of GDP at constant prices, reached a new peak of 27.1 per cent, exceeding the previous peak of 25.9 per cent in 1990—91. Gross fixed capital formation which is even more important for productivity and growth, reached a new peak of 24.1 per cent of GDP in 1995—96. Private sector investment appears to have responded vigorously to the policy of promoting competition, removing policy distortions and hurdles, and improving access to factors of production (e.g. technology, capital).

Estimates of savings and investment in 1996—97 are not yet available. Indicators are mixed. On the one hand, domestic capital goods production is buoyent and disbursement of financial institutions are significantly higher, on the other hand, capital goods imports have declined, non—oil imports are lower in the first nine months of the year, corporate demand for credit appears slack, and sanctions of financial institutions are substantially lower.

The economy in 1996—97 so far presents a mixed picture in other dimensions as well. Although overall economic growth remains high at 6.8 per cent, and agriculture has rebounded, the growth of manufacturing value added has slowed and the performance of key infrastructure sectors, especially power and crude oil, is weak. The annual rate of inflation (point to point) has risen back to average long—term levels and export growth has decelerated markedly in recent months. Despite the slowdown in exports, a combination of sluggish imports and reasonably buoyant inflows of invisibles and capital flows have led to a build—up of foreign exchange reserves by over $ 2.5 billion.

Agriculture and Indian economy

The Economic Survey–1996—97 is a balanced appraisal of the past performance of the economy, attributing the gains to the policy of economic reform and liberalisaton, pursued during the last five years and presents a picture of cautious optimism for the future. While attributing the past gains to the policy of liberalisation, the Survey asserts that the policy would need to be pursued with greater vigour in future to carry the economy to higher growth path. It attributes "the loss of momentum" in the economy to "the marked slow down in the pace of reforms preceding and during the election period", but adds "this has been revived with a series of measures in recent months."

The Survey says "the initial spurt of reforms from 1991—92 t 1993—94 was very successful on all accounts, resulting in a jump in economic growth in 1994—95 to 7.2 per cent." It says GDP grew by 7.1 per cent in 1995—96 despite the slowdown in the momentum of reform and adds, econmic growth in 1996—97 is estimated by the CSO to be around 6.8 per cent (GDP at factor cost). The Eight Plan, it says is thus likely to end with an average growth of 6.5 per cent per annum, 0.9 per cent higher than the target rate of 5.6 per cent and 0.5 per cent point higher than the actual achievement of the Seventh Plan. More important for the future is the fact that the average growth during the latest three years is 7 per cent, probably placing India among the top ten performers in the world during the period." However, when it comes to a review of sectoral performance that he Survey is compelled to be more realistic. It says "the economy in 1996–97 so far presents a mixed picture." Although, it says "overall economic growth remains high at 6.8 per cent, and agriculture has rebounded, the growth of manufacturing value added has slowed and the performance of key infrastructure sectors, especially power and crude oil, is weak. The annual rate of inflation (point to point) has risen t actual long—term levels and export growth has decelerated markedly in recent months."

On agriculture, the Survey says "production in 1996—97 is expected to show good recovery from the slower growth in 1995—96. The growth is projected at 3 per cent after a fall of 0.4 per cent in 1995–96. The sharp decline in foodgrains production by 3.4 per cent, which was responsible for the slow growth in 1995–96, is expected to be reversed by; an increase of 3.3 per cent in 1996—97. Foodgrains production is expected to recover to 191.2 million tonnes, only marginally lower than the level of production in 1994—95. The recovery is primarily due to coarse cereals, as well as anticipated rise in wheat production, which suffered a sharp setback in 1995—96." Commercial crop production has done extremely well in 1996—97 with oilseeds and cotton expected to reach record levels of 24.1 and 14.1 million tonnes respectively.

In the previous chapter, we described the situation as it prevailed in 1960-61. We shall now proceed to take a brief review of the progress made during the past decade. The last year for which some data are available is 1968-69. Therefore, in the following review, we shall cover the period from 1960-61 to 1968-69.

National Income again offers a useful summary measure to judge the performance of the economy in a given period. The particular measure of national income we shall use is specifically termed Net National Product at Factor Cost. We shall briefly refer to it as NNP. We have earlier mentioned that the NNP was Rs. 13,308 crores in 1960-61. It increased to Rs. 28,800 crores in 1968-69 was 216.4. The NNP increased annually by about 6 percentage points during 1961-62 and 1962-63; by almost 17 percentage points in 1963-64; by 26 percentage points in the next two years; by 23 percentage points in 1966-67; by 32 percentage points in 1967-68; and finally, by 6 percentage points in 1968-69. Over the eight years from 1960-61 to 1968-69, the NNP more than doubled.

This is a spectacular performance if it were all real. Unfortunately it is not all real. During the eight years from 1960-61 to 1968-69, the prices of commodities have almost doubled. This means that a rupee in 1968-69 does not mean the same thing as it did in 1960-61. Hence, to judge the real increase in NNP, we should ask what would the NNP be if the prices had remained unchanged. In other words, we should value the NNP in subsequent years at prices as they prevailed in 1960-61. We shall refer to this as Net National Product at Constant (1960-61) Prices. From such a series, it becomes clear that the NNP increased by only 26.5 per cent in eight years and not by 116.4 per cnet as appeared earlier. Thus the real increase in the NNP is only 26.5 per cent in eight years; the balance of apparent increase is a reflection of the increase in prices.

The growth in the NNP has not been steady. This is because agricultural production, which constitutes almost half of the total, is still liable to wide fluctuations from year to year. The real increase in the NNP by 6 percentage points in 1963-64 and again by 8 percentage points in 1964-65 was because of the good agricultural season in those two years. This was followed by two very bad years and the NNP actually declined in 1965-66 and remained at the same low level in 1966-67. Fortunately, the year 1967-68 turned out to be a very good year and the NNP jumped by 10 percentage points. The year 1968-69 was also a good year and the NNP is estimated to have advanced by another 2 percentage points.

Thus the anunal fluctuations in agricultural production explain the unsteady growth of the NNP. But in a period as long as 8 to 10 years, one must take good years along with bad years and reckon the fact that the real increase in NNP in eight years was only 26.5 per cent which is a compound growth rate of less than 3 per cent per annum.

The growth in the NNP must be placed alongside the growth in population. The population of the Indian Union in 1961 was 434 million. We shall know what it is when the census is taken this year. However, in the meanwhile, the population is estimated to have been growing at the annual rate of 2.5 per cent. Clearly, therefore, a growth of NNP at an annual rate of no more than 3 per cent is barely sufficient to keep pace with the growth in population; it leaves little margin to make a net improvement in the economic condition of the people. This becomes clear if we divide the NNP by the estimated population each year to get the NNP per capita. If this is done, it becomes clear that the per capita NNP increased from Rs. 306.7 in 1960-61 to just Rs. 321.3 in 1967-68 and Rs. 319.4 in 1968-69. This is an increase at best of only 4.5 per cent in eight years which is about half a per cent per annum. This summarises the performance of the economy during the past decade.

As mentioned earlier, per capita private consumer expenditure gives a more direct measure of the well-being or standard of living of a people. We have seen that the per capita private consumer expenditure was Rs. 276.3 in 1960-61. In are given the relevant data for the subsequent years. In order to assess the real changes in the per capita consumer expenditure in subsequent years at constant (1960-61) prices for the years from 1960-61 to 1968-69.

It will be seen that the per capita consumer expenditure increased from Rs. 276.3 in 1960-61 to Rs. 285.5 (at 1960-61 prices) in 1968-69. The per capita consumer expenditure shows a sudden increase (Rs. 296.0) in 1964-65 and then a sudden fall (Rs. 269.8 and Rs. 271.8) in the following two years. This is a reflection of the bumper agricultural production in 1964-65 and poor production in the following two years. The average per capita consumption during the three years 1964-65, 1965-66 and 1966-67 was Rs. 279.2 per annum. It seems more likely that the real consumption was maintained more or less at this level by carrying some of the large stocks of 1964-65 into the next two years rather than allowing it to fluctuate along with fluctuations in agricultural production. For the same reason, we should smoothen out the fluctuations in the first three years as also in the last two years. When this is done, the estimates of per capita consumer expenditure in the nine years appear as shown in. They seem more reasonable and plausible.

The upshot of the whole exercise is that the per capita consumer expenditure rose from Rs. 276.3 in 1960-61 to Rs. 289.6 in 1968-69, that is by 4.8 per cent in eight years or by about half a per cent per annum. It is obvious that it could not have risen by any more because, we have seen as the per capita income rose at best by 4.5 per cent in the eight years.

Incidentally, we may note that the per capita consumer expenditure seems to have increased a little more than has the per capita national income. The reasons seem to be firstly that the large increase in national income registered in the last two years has been mainly on account of the large increase in the production of foodgrains in these years and secondly that the net domestic capital formation as a proportion of the net domestic expenditure has gone down sharply in these two years.

This brings us to the next point namely how are these small gains of development distributed between different sections of the population–between the rural and urban populations and between the richer and poorer sections of these populations? More specifically, we ask: The average consumer expenditure in the country rose by 4.8 per cent in real terms (that is at constant prices) in the eight years from 1960-61 and 1968-69. Did this happen equally in the case of the rural and urban populations and equally in the case of the richer and poorer sections of these populations? These questions are crucial while assessing whether anything is happening to the poor of this country; whether their lot has improved materially as a result of the economic development of the past decade. If the per capita consumption in the country has risen by no more than 4.8 per cent in eight years, it is obvious that little noticeable could have happened in the nature of alleviation of poverty unless the poorer sections have profited proportionately more than the average and much more so than the rich.